How to Tell If Your Teenager Is Lying
and What to Do about It

How to Tell If Your Teenager Is Lying

and What to Do about It

Alan R. Hirsch, M.D., F.A.C.P.

HILTON PUBLISHING

© 2010 by Hilton Publishing Company, Indianapolis, IN

Grant E. Mabie, *Managing Editor*
Lynn Bell, *Editorial Assistance*
Debby Dutton, Dutton & Sherman Design, *Layout & Design*

Direct all correspondence to:
Hilton Publishing Company
816 Fort Wayne Avenue
Indianapolis, IN 46204
317–602–8090
www.hiltonpub.com

ISBN 978–0–9800649–0–2

Notice: The information in this book is true and complete to the best of the author's and publisher's knowledge. This book is intended only as an informative reference and should not replace, countermand, or conflict with the advice given to readers by their physicians. The authors and publisher disclaim all liability in connection with the specific personal use of any and all information provided in this book. References to real people, events, establishments, organizations, or locales are intended only to provide a sense of authenticity and are used fictitiously.

Library of Congress Cataloging-in-Publication Data

Hirsch, Alan R.
    How to Tell If Your Teenager Is Lying and What to Do about It / Alan R. Hirsch.
        p. cm.
    ISBN 978–0–9800649–0–2
    1. Truthfulness and falsehood in adolescence. 2. Child rearing. I. Title.
    BF724.3.T78H57 2008
    155.5'18—dc22   2007048898

Printed and bound in the United States of America

To my mother, who, through her actions, has taught me the real meaning of truth, perseverance, and commitment.

Other Books by the Author

Hirsch, A. R. *Sensa Weight-Loss Program: The Accidental Discovery That's Transforming the Way People Lose Weight.* Chicago: Hilton Publishing, 2009.

Hirsch, A. R. *What's Your FOOD SIGN? How to Use Food Clues to Find Lasting Love.* New York: Stewart, Tabori & Chang, 2006.

Hirsch, A. R. *What Your Doctor May Not Tell You about Sinusitis: Release Your Symptoms and Identify the Real Source of Your Pain.* New York: Warner Books, 2004.

Hirsch, A. R. *Life's a Smelling Success: Using Scent to Empower Your Memory and Learning.* Mt. Shasta, Calif.: Unity Publishing, 2003.

Hirsch, A. R. *What Flavor Is Your Personality? Discover Who You Are by Looking at What You Eat.* Naperville, Ill.: Sourcebooks, Inc., 2001.

Hirsch, A. R. *Scentsational Sex: The Secret to Using Aroma for Arousal.* Boston: Element Books, 1998.

Hirsch, A. R. *Dr. Hirsch's Guide to Scentsational Weight Loss.* Rockport, Mass.: Element Books, 1997.

Contents

Acknowledgments

Ben Sweetland observed, "Success is a journey, not a destination." It is with sincerest gratitude that I wish to acknowledge those who have helped me in this quest. Penultimate is Denise Fahey and Michele Soto, truly kalogathical without their long hours of selfless devotion, this project would never have come to fruition.

Kudos to the insightful guidance of Dr. H. Hudson II, who had the foresight and vision to undertake and share in this expedition.

To Noah Lukeman and Virginia McCullough, whose balladromic guidance avoided any withershins roaming.

And, to Noah, Camryn, Jack, Marissa, and bellibone, Debra, who serve as inspiration for life's journey.

Alan R. Hirsch, M.D.
September 2010

Foreword

I am honored to be asked to write the foreword for Dr. Hirsch's latest book, *How to Tell If Your Teenager Is Lying*.

I have had the pleasure of knowing Alan Hirsch for almost 20 years now, since my clinical years of medical school in Chicago. Dr. Hirsch was known as a "Doogie Howser*," because he entered medical school at an age when most of us were still in high school, and had double-board certification in a unique combination of brain specialty areas (neurology and psychiatry).

Dr. Hirsch's elective rotation in neurology was a popular choice amongst my medical school classmates. He was a sought-after teacher because he was informative and educational, but also offered a true taste (pun intended) of clinical practice in an exciting office-based practice and with a unique patient population. Even then, Dr. Hirsch was known for his expertise in the areas of smell and taste. His large practice, academic affiliations, and boundless energy often meant the possibility for participation in a research

---

* '80s/early '90s TV comedy-drama.

project, and even the ultimate of all medical student resumé boosters . . . publication!

Needless to say, I jumped at every opportunity Dr. Hirsch offered, and have been collaborating with him ever since. I was unsure of my choice of medical specialty, and Dr. Hirsch's mentoring and excitement about his work were definite contributors to my eventual decision to undertake specialty training in psychiatry, to think scientifically, and to pursue life and medicine with passion. My work with Alan has generally focused on the crossover between neurology (specifically taste and smell) and psychiatry, an area expanding in the scientific literature.

I fondly remember working late into the night at Dr. Hirsch's Michigan Avenue office, which sometimes carried over to the hotel lobby next door, where he bought a poor medical student a beer while he sipped coffee and complained that I had a "soporific" effect on him (definition—causing sleep; tending to cause sleep).

Since that time, Alan has continued his studies of the complexities of human behavior, often intertwined with the neuropsychiatric complexities of chemosensation (the perception of smell and taste). As a colleague and a psychiatrist, I have watched with interest as Dr. Hirsch has tackled topical issues in modern culture (sexuality, weight loss, sales and marketing impact) from the unique perspective of smell and taste. I am further impressed with the way Dr. Hirsch continues to pursue psychiatric issues in his quest for scientific knowledge and understanding. Despite a prolific career as an author, I believe this book is the most direct evidence of Dr. Hirsch's training in psychiatry, and displays his understanding of human behavior and relationships. Particularly, this book provides advocacy for the basic human needs for family and parenting—which makes this child psychiatrist proud!

There are several references to interesting and thought provoking studies that involve deception and interpretion of human behavior, including correlations with . . . the nose! Even though this book provides much information about the roots and dynamics underlying deception, I believe the strongest message is in the delicate exploration of the parent-child relationship throughout development, and Dr. Hirsch's passionate advocacy of parental involvement and defense of the family as a priority in our society. Alan's anecdotal insight into his own family adds a personal touch to a book that, at times, provides sophisticated neurobiological information, and then counters with psychodynamic theories of human behavior and parenting. There are many basic relationship-building tips, including suggestions and strategies to communicate more effectively with your child. Dr. Hirsch gives parents advice to help detect deception and, more importantly, explores the various situations that may lead to this type of behavior, with options and suggestions for response and intervention.

Throughout, Dr. Hirsch emphasizes the importance of involved parenting, open communication, and the overriding need for priority of family in society. Dr. Hirsch has always incorporated his psychiatric background into his work with smell and taste, which is what makes his prior studies and publications so unique and interesting. This book represents a slight shift from Dr. Hirsch's traditional focus on chemosensation, and instead, the focus is on human behavior. This former student welcomes the emphasis on Alan's other area of expertise, including his explorations into the complexities of parenting.

Thomas J. Trannel, M.D.
Board Certified, Psychiatry
Board Certified, Child and Adolescent Psychiatry
University of Illinois, Chicago College of Medicine, Class of 1991

Introduction

If you're a parent, you desperately need this book. I know that's a strong statement, but I mean it. Frankly, I'm a parent, and I know how much my wife and I need—and constantly remind ourselves about—the information presented in the chapters ahead.

Probably no age group is more enthusiastic and passionate about their interests and beliefs than teenagers. No one stands up for a political candidate or the need to "save the planet" or help the less fortunate better than "tuned-in" teenagers, especially the closer they get to voting age. Today's kids constantly hear platitudes about being "the future," and we encourage them to take stands and make their voices heard. (Well, up to a point!)

Sometimes, teenagers' very awkwardness and sensitivity and their still playful and humorous tendencies endear adults. The joy and pain of first jobs, first dates, and first love draw us adults in and may trigger memories, both good and perhaps not so good. Parenting a teen can allow us to vicariously reexperience the exuberance of youth, and empathize with his frustrations and disappointments at the same time. Most teens experience at least a few bumps in the road, and few are fortunate enough to sail smoothly through these years.

As much as we love our teens and want to enjoy them as they go through this final stage of childhood, we may also want to pull our hair out in frustration. Turmoil, almost constant conflict, deep hurts, mood swings—all these terms describe the turbulent adolescent years, too, and they often apply to both parents and teens. Parents may be disappointed in their kids during this last phase of childhood in which many teens violate long-held family rules by getting into trouble in school or in myriad other ways. Likewise, kids must cope with disappointment as they struggle to make their way in what we can accurately call "teen society." For many parents, these years are, at best, a roller coaster of emotions.

Too often, parents are unaware that their children have psychologically strayed from the family system, to use a sociological term, and now identify with their peers to the exclusion of parents, teachers, and other adults. In some families, rather than observing their kids with a mix of concern and amusement, the parents live in an anxious state, having sensed that their teens are off living in their own "tribe" and speaking an unfamiliar tongue.

The pre-adolescent and teen years represent the time that our children are exposed to so much so fast—most parents say "way too fast." Before these years, parents usually shelter their children as much as possible, even though that's a difficult task today. We view our kids as novices at the business of life and not mature enough to understand or handle adult concerns. The kids often think they're very mature and ready to handle making adult choices, and this is why communication often breaks down. Sometimes common ground is hard to find.

Today's kids, like those of past generations, must learn to set a course that allows them to survive the seductive, but potentially dangerous, temptations the world holds. At the very least, they're exposed to cigarette smoking and alcohol, and, almost certainly, illegal drugs. Earlier than ever, they're confronted with the lure of sexual activity that, at minimum, puts them at risk for pregnancy and sexually transmitted diseases. This early exposure to the power of their sexuality may ultimately lead to a promiscuous lifestyle. Day after day, the pressure is on to step outside the boundaries of good judgment and morals.

It's true that some people find the discussion of teens and the kinds of risks to which they're exposed difficult and painful. Given a choice, all parents would prefer to concentrate on the positive side of adolescent life and try to reap the benefits of the years of hard work they've already invested instilling morals and values. Our challenge as parents is to strike a balance between loosening our hold in some areas, while hanging on tight in others. We want to foster independence and enjoy a close relationship, while exercising judgment and caution, and by reining our adolescents in when necessary.

Every period of life has its risks, but the teenage years bring us special worries because the risks are potentially so dangerous. For example, drug use during this critical period of brain development causes permanent, irreversible damage to the brain, specifically to two areas known as the nucleus accumbens and the frontal cortex, which are involved in motivation and "higher executive function." These functions include decision-making, evaluating information and situations, and planning for the future.

Based on current brain research, a single exposure to a variety of psychotropic drugs during the teen years (especially before the age of 17 or 18) can adversely affect the rest of the teenager's life. (More about this later.)

As loving parents, our role, before all else, is to provide safety and protection for our offspring. But it's no exaggeration to say that we live in a drug-infested, morally bankrupt society—across all socio-economic, ethnic, and racial lines. Regardless of their circumstances, all parents fight uphill battles.

Just think of what the pressure to be "cool" and part of the "in crowd" meant a few generations ago. We know that, for many, it meant sneaking cigarettes—often their parents' cigarettes. That particular temptation was and is dangerous. It may be the single most dangerous thing that young people of the past engaged in because it led to a range of diseases that still overwhelm our healthcare system today. But, as our grandparents would correctly point out, it isn't cigarette smoking that leads to anti-social behavior—fights, impaired driving, and casual sexuality.

With the exception of cigarette smoking, however, being cool was less dangerous several decades ago than it is today. Maybe cool meant wearing leather jackets, or growing long hair, or swallowing goldfish! It might have meant boys sneaking a can of beer or two when they hung out together on a Friday night. For girls, it might have meant putting on heavy makeup or hiking up their skirts after they left the house. While the teens may have thought of themselves as a separate group, they were accountable to others, and their "intra-tribal" behavior—and language—had limits. They visited this strange universe they created, but they didn't live there.

Most of today's parents were adolescents during the turbulent '70s, '80s, and early '90s, or, perhaps the late '60s. Given the exposure to drugs and alcohol and early sexual activity many parents experienced, it's difficult to understand how any among them could bury their heads in the sand about the atmosphere for teenagers today. Even as kids, today's parents understood that the idea of swallowing goldfish or secretly adding more makeup as devious behavior belonged to yesteryear. In fact, many of today's parents have experience with the designer drugs and casual sexuality that mystified their parents. Now, they may be overly concerned about their teens because of their own involvement in what was essentially a teen life they worked hard to keep hidden from their own parents.

It can be difficult to believe, but today's kids face even more risky behaviors, and, because of sophisticated media and communications, they may be "hyper-aware" of sexual matters and of alcohol and drugs much earlier than even their parents. Being "cool" might mean sniffing dangerous inhalants as a pre-teen, casually using profanity in public, stealing alcohol from parents, using crack cocaine, or risking contracting hepatitis and HIV from unprotected—not to mention ill-advised—sexual activities. For girls, it might mean videotaping themselves topless or performing some kind of "exotic" dance. Sadly, these videos may end up on the Internet.

These activities may be cool to the A students as well as the barely-scraping-by kids. Even worse, in some circles and communities, being cool still means doing poorly in school—being an achiever may be okay at age 10, but it may be socially isolating at age 15.

Today, we could say that "cool" almost always is synonymous with "risk." Current risks and temptations have infiltrated all levels of society, especially in virtually all U.S. secondary schools and many junior-high or middle schools. I call this infusion of risky behavior part of a more general moral decline (and decline in morale) that has eroded the innocence of American youth. What once was wholly unacceptable and intolerable is now the norm.

Fifty years ago, using profanity or sexually charged language in school would likely have led to some kind of disciplinary action or even suspension. Even thirty years ago, this kind of behavior was considered notable, if not ultimately treated as behavior that required discipline. Of course, this varied from region to region and school to school. However, if you take a walk through the halls of most high schools anywhere in the country, you will hear language that even the teachers will tell you is so common but it is not even given notice. Besides, the teachers and administrators must contend with problems so much more serious that students using profanity seems like the least of them!

Granted, these problems aren't new. According to the Department of Education's Center for Education Sciences, incidents of school violence and theft have decreased since reaching a peak in the 1990s. However, we can't ignore that in 2005, 1.2 million reported incidents of crime, including theft and non-fatal assaults, occurred among children ages 12 to 18 in their schools. Crime of any kind is of concern because it threatens the sense of wellbeing in the school community. Crime aside, the fact that school administrators and teachers have to pick their battles and avoid confronting kids over language, revealing clothing and even skipping school altogether tells us that the breakdown of standards has reached a critical point. When has skipping school not been considered truancy, a giant step toward what we used to call delinquency? Have we cut resources in schools used to detect and track down absent kids and reduced the consequences for not showing up to the point that some school districts can barely assess the problem?

Most parents shake their heads in disgust at the behavior that celebrities model for our kids, from heavy drinking and using illicit drugs (and driving under the influence) to blatant sexual promiscuity. It seems that our airwaves are jammed with reports of one more famous teen or young-adult in jail or rehab, or both. Tragically, privileged celebrity teens and young adults may not pay the same consequences for their bad behavior as the typical teen. In other words, the average teenage alcoholic-addict won't get the chance to go to an upscale rehab center and instead, may end up in juvenile detention.

So, yes, as parents we must acknowledge that the acceptable standard of today, at least in much of society, is the unacceptable standard of yesterday. The moral component is one thing, but putting that aside, these acceptable behaviors are dangerous to the very lives of our children. At minimum, they pay a physical price for risky behavior, and they may harm themselves permanently.

As parents, we also face the realization that we can go on and on about the "downfall of society," and bemoan the end of civilization as we know it, but in the end, we can truly only control what goes on in our own families. We can try to influence the world around us and voice our concerns. We can take up a crusade to rid the neighborhood of drugs or pornography, or we can join various movements to discourage teen drinking and driving. We can demand greater safety measures in our schools and become active volunteer parents to monitor progress. Doing all that doesn't change the reality that we must keep close watch on what happens in our own homes.

I look at what's happened in our culture and the many losses to individuals and to our society as a kind of "Vietnam War" of casualties—children injured and dying from sexually transmitted diseases (STDs), drugs, auto and motorcycle accidents, alcohol poisoning and other alcohol-related injuries, and so forth. While this isn't a book about teenage drinking or sexual activity among teens, I'm not exaggerating when I say that teens are at serious risk. Here are just a handful of reports and statistics:

- In March of 2008, NPR reported the results of a study showing that 25% of teenage girls in the U.S. are infected with one of four commons STDs: human papilloma virus (HPV), herpes, chlamydia, or trichomoniasis. You notice that this list doesn't include HIV, gonorrhea, or syphilis; in fact, half of all HIV infections in the U.S. occur among those under age 25.

- About 50% of all drowning deaths in teens are related to alcohol abuse and is a major cause of death in teen auto accidents.

- Teen alcohol users are more likely to become sexually active at earlier ages, have sexual intercourse more often, and have unprotected sex than their peers who do not drink.

- Teens and young adults who drink are more likely than others to be victims of violent crime, including rape, aggravated assault, and other related crimes.

- Those who begin drinking as young teens are four times more likely to develop alcohol dependence than someone who waits until adulthood to use alcohol.

The bar has been raised in that age-old adolescent imperative to revolt and engage in shocking behavior. We see the biggest change in the degree to which rebellious behavior can cause serious harm or even lead to death. Swallowing goldfish and getting a stomachache doesn't compare to crack cocaine–induced stroke.

Despite this bad news, we can't make adolescent revolt go away. It's linked to human nature and, in one form or another, even to the survival of the species. Adolescents, in gaining their identities, must break away from their parents, rejecting their values and embracing those of their friends and those idealized "parents" they see on television and on the Internet. As parents, we must understand that our kids' rejection of us doesn't mean that they hate or despise us.

No, it's not that simple, because rebellion is a step in the natural process of generational separation—it's growth in action. Without this developmental stage, troubling and stressful though it is, teenagers would never become fully functioning and independent men and women.

As school-children, you probably saw films about nature and animal behavior. You may recall the nurturing behavior of a mother bear, for example, and her fierce protection of her cubs. Yet, when they were old enough to survive on their own, she left them behind. You may have seen adult birds literally push their young out of the nest to teach them to fly, another example of Mother Nature's tough love. Without that behavior, the species would die out.

The teen years are the final phase of preparing our human young to leave our nests. We are caught in an in-between stage, too. We want them to develop independence, yet we must protect them from the impulse to take leaps before they know how to fly. We need to leave them alone to make mistakes and survive them, but we have to be within shouting distance, too, and provide the safety nets they may still need. It's tough and getting tougher in these days of blurry standards and rules; with natural but frustrating rebellion.

However, all is not lost. As a parent, you have options. You can do things to modulate and mold this rebellious response to a more "socially acceptable" rejection of your standards and norms. Or, put another way, our teens might declare themselves Republicans in our Democratic households or vice versa. We can live with that! What we don't want to see is sociopathic acting out such as shoplifting at the mall while tripping on drugs or taking a dare and engaging in casual, but risky sexual behavior.

As discussed later on, the absolute best way to steer your teenagers towards socially acceptable rebellion is to guide them to the right circle of friends, rather than "make-believe friends," the music icons and the characters kids tend to find in TV programs and movies. However, even with the best of friends, you'll likely encounter situations where a question arises about the exact nature of your teenager's behavior. Was there alcohol at the party? Who is sniffing what, and where did they get it? Why do their clothes smell like the Woodstock concert? What are the pills in the plastic bag? Why did your son miss two classes last week? How long has your daughter been carrying around condoms in her backpack? (Perhaps the more important questions are: "Does my daughter understand the range of STDs for which condoms do not offer protection? Is her education about sex and STDs thorough and complete and not limited to preventing pregnancy?") Did your son join in the rampage after the football game or run away to avoid it? Was the speed limit law broken or was the fender bender a true accident, and, if so, how did it happen?

When these questions come up, as they most certainly will, how can you tell if your teenager is responding truthfully? Being able to determine a truthful or deceptive statement becomes essential, and potentially, may even save your teenager's life. This will allow you to separate your teen from the crowd or initiate plans to further modify her behavior, depending on the situation. Maybe grounding the teen for a week or two matches the infraction and is tough enough. But, under certain circumstances, sending your child to drug rehabilitation might be the life-saving measure you must take.

This book provides some of the tools you can use to distinguish the lying from the truthful teenager. These are weapons that support your fight for the health, happiness, and safety of your children during a most vulnerable stage, adolescence. To put this in technical terms, during these years brain function has not achieved the full maturation required for cognition not superseded by emotion.

In everyday language, this means that teens tend to let emotional impulses, the desire and the lure of excitement, take over and wipe away better judgment. When we ask teens, "What were you thinking?" in our incredulous parental voice, we are often met with a blank stare. They might as well tell us that they weren't thinking at all!

We adults aren't immune, by the way. We often are sorely tempted to let our emotions take over—frankly, illicit love affairs usually happen when emotion supersedes cognition. Over-spending and falling into debt are rampant today among supposedly wise and educated adults. Given the economic realities we face today, our children need to understand that we may be re-learning money management strategies and will pass on the pair of shoes or set of golf clubs that strains our budget. Mature adults usually face and deal with this predicament, perhaps returning the item or cutting back somewhere else—or accept that we've added the money to our credit card debt. I'm afraid that many parents are facing up to the fact that they are not mature enough when it comes to material things.

So often in my medical practice, those I counsel who have acted on emotion, usually rage—a heightened states of emotional arousal—ultimately regret it. But reasonably mature adults in their right minds, meaning not drunk or drugged or mentally ill, have the capacity to choose the logical option over the irrational, emotionally-driven one.

We must understand that because of developmental issues, teenagers face a particular challenge in choosing the logical over the irrational, and that leads to unwise decisions. This is analogous to the "tired brain," the midnight or the 3:00 AM brain that caves into basic emotional drives over a response rooted in reason. This is why logical, but overtired adults may hunt through the kitchen cabinets looking for cookies or chips, for example. All their knowledge about a good diet goes out the window when the brain is tired. This is also why otherwise cautious adults may engage in unsafe sexual practices late at night.

When the brain is tired, the limbic system (the primitive or emotional brain) takes over, and cerebral cortex functions (the "thinking" part of the brain) are suppressed. We see evidence of this when we consider the increase in emergency room visits as a result of violent crimes, including domestic violence, that take place in the wee hours of the morning.

So, whether we like it or not, we must not resist or deny that these same emotion-driven decisions confront our teenagers at every turn. Of course, sometimes even among kids, emotion succumbs to logic, but often it doesn't, and that's when disastrous results follow, especially today when the risks are so great and so numerous.

Given all the risky behaviors our children have access to, it becomes especially important to know when your teenager is lying or telling the truth. By studying this single area, you will take back the reins, so to speak. You will be back in control of the safety and health of your child.

This subject is not without controversy. Certainly, some believe that it isn't fair to use techniques other than simply trusting your child, to determine whether he or she is lying. But I urge these conflicted parents to reconsider. I suggest that the most compassionate— and responsible—thing parents can do is protect their children from harm, especially when that harm is self-induced.

But, some ask, is it possible to go too far in protecting your child? As a parent myself, I can say that, short of restricting children from any association with the outside world or engaging in abuse, there is no such thing as too far. Use all the tools and techniques available to you to provide for your child's safety. Certainly, keep doing all the typical things parents do as they raise their children in all kinds of conditions. If possible, move to a better, safer neighborhood. Save for a good college and do your best to provide a physically and emotionally safe home environment. And use your knowledge of human behavior to accurately read and respond to your teenager. In so doing, you will have maximized his chance of growing to become a productive, independent adult.

So in this book I present a process that enhances your capacity to determine if your teenager is lying, along with advice about preventing deceptive behavior. This "lie detection" program is based on interviewing and non-physical interrogating techniques used in psychiatry, law enforcement, and the military. In allowing you to understand your adolescent, these tools become as important for you as they are in the fields in which they were developed. Using these tools properly may not only help you keep your child out of trouble, but also healthy and well as she passes through these difficult adolescent years. Ultimately, your child will thank you for your wisdom—and for your determination to keep him or her safe and unharmed, even from his or her own dangerous or ill-advised impulses.

Chapter 1

Everybody Lies

Your teenager is a great liar. You have yourself to thank for that. Like all of your child's behavior, your Suzy or Sam has learned to lie from you. It's like the adage in the Bible, "You reap what you sow." Day in and day out, our teens have watched us tell little white lies, the ones we call lies of convenience, or even the lie of stealing, and have incorporated them into their own ethics and values. The lies go something like this:

"I'll play with you after the basketball game on TV is over."

"We'll stop at the toy store tomorrow."

"We'll go to the movies later."

And, assuming for the sake of discussion that you don't follow through, these lies teach your disappointed child not only how to lie, but that lying is morally acceptable, an okay way to wiggle out of commitments or cover up a mistake. Of course, lies come in different forms and degrees of seriousness, but remember, your child learns them all from his environment.

I know a lawyer I'll call Mark. He always drives through toll booths without paying. Other than this lapse, he's a well respected professional and family man with high moral standards. He'd never consider picking a pocket or embezzling from his firm, yet paying at the toll booths doesn't hold any moral value for him. So where did his attitude come from? I mulled this over for years, until I happened upon the answer in a discussion with his fourteen-year-old child, who mentioned that his grandfather never paid tolls either. Aha! Mark learned this behavior from his father, and since his father acted as if this was proper and right, Mark has adopted these same ideals and values, and never pays tolls. Now the same behavior is being passed on to a third generation. So "toll booth immorality" is every bit as much a part of the family's profile as "Thou shall not break and enter a home and steal valuables." Mark doesn't even see not paying his tolls as deviant behavior—it's not a setting on his moral compass.

Families set the tone in other ways, too. Why, for example, do some people ignore certain conventions, like cleaning up their own tables in fast-food restaurants or putting their shopping carts in the designated spot in the supermarket parking lot? For various reasons, some people don't see these conventions as relevant to them. These small lifestyle attitudes and differences set people apart, and kids usually follow suit. Although these don't seem like serious moral concerns, they are part of an ethical pattern that govern the way a family and its members behave.

Creating a Moral Compass

Where does a moral compass come from? For some, it's based on religious doctrine—perhaps the Ten Commandments or a similar religious code. For others, it's family-based or perhaps even rooted in long-held traditions about what keeps families, clans, tribes, city-states, and countries going. But what happens if a person lacks such a moral compass? In that case, the prohibition of behaviors such as lying or stealing won't be based on that person's internal judgment of right or wrong, but rather, on external factors. Things like social pressures, laws and their enforcement, the looming threat of punishment, and the odds of getting caught begin to influence decisions.

Increasingly, our society has drifted away from formal religious doctrine and towards a more secular vision, which, for many, means that the moral compass has become fuzzy. (More on this in later chapters.) Without an absolute system of morality established through religion or another strong ethical code, then children absorb moral values based on their exposure to the "Big Four":

- parents,

- television,

- peers, and

- school.

If the commandment against lying is erased, then we enter areas in which it's okay to lie for convenience or personal gain. This becomes acceptable behavior, without carrying the weight of guilt or shame. When this happens, the truth is hollow and devoid of absolute value. Social intercourse, historically based on mutual trust, breaks down, ultimately replaced with "mutual distrust."

Where Do You Stand?

So when is it okay to lie? Not ever? For self-gain? For convenience? Out of loyalty? To protect a loved one? To spare another person's feelings?

Most agree that it's okay for a spy to lie. We view that as patriotism, and deception goes with the territory. Most of us see the so-called "white lie" as part of what lubricates social interaction. We tell our host that inedible food was "fantastic," and let's face it, not every bride and every new grandchild is "sooo beautiful."

These social white lies are considered altruistic lying, and children pick up on the fact that we consider this form of lying acceptable, even laudable. We all absorb the idea that these lies promote happiness in others, so even the very religious promote the empathic lie. In an old story, a man confronts a rabbi about calling a bride "beautiful," although it's clear she's quite homely by any standard. Brushing away the criticism of his "lie," the rabbi explains, "She is beautiful on the inside." In a larger context, it's probably true that "love is blind" and the objects of our affection, whether they're spouses, children, or dogs, are beautiful, even if others think us daffy.

By contrast, lying for self-serving purposes is viewed in a negative light. Telling a woman she's the most beautiful person in the room is an immoral lie if the compliment is a prelude to trying to marry her for her fortune.

Sometimes situations are more complex than they first seem, and lying by omission may be viewed as morally acceptable. In general, passive actions carry less moral weight than those we'd call active. In terms of lying, a lie of omission is considered more morally acceptable than an active lie. We see this in situations in which ignoring the truth or remaining silent can be considered morally acceptable. It's one thing if your child sees someone stealing something or cheating on a test, but chooses not to speak up and be labeled a tattletale or a snitch. But if the child is questioned about the theft or cheating incident and makes up false statements, then the deception is considered more morally serious.

Sometimes, withholding information for the purpose of deception puts active and passive lying on equal moral planes. To use
a famous example, the world listened while former President Bill
Clinton, who faced impeachment over his affair with a White
House intern, gave his testimony to a special prosecutor appointed
by the Attorney General. It's universally agreed that this was a particularly embarrassing display by a leader. For example, he split hairs
over the meaning of "is," saying in response to a question, "That
depends on what the meaning of 'is' is." This suggested his intent to
obfuscate the whole truth about the timing of what had occurred. In
other words, he attempted to hide behind the literal truth in order
to cover up the spirit of the truth. (More on Bill Clinton in a later
chapter.)

Yet adults, even presidents and prime ministers and kings—and
that thirteen-year-old living in your house—feel superior when they
pull off this kind of trickery. It's not that different from shoplifters
who outwit the shopkeeper and then brag about it. They may show
great hubris while lying and revel in their superior intellect and chi-
canery.

When teenagers can fool you with their lies, especially those of
omission, they may feel good, even confident, because you are an
authority figure, the equivalent of storekeeper, teacher, police offi-
cer, and so forth. Getting away with such trickery makes them feel
strong and powerful. And since they withheld information, they
haven't technically violated the moral code of "thou shalt not lie."

Those feelings of power wave at us like red flags, because they
are based on a warped moral code. Parents have to understand what
children pick up from this kind of deception. For better or worse,
our society has allowed this lying loophole to be accepted—it's the
moral equivalent of the "get out of jail free" card in Monopoly. We
unwittingly encourage deception without the guilt of dishonesty.

Teenagers need to learn that if telling the partial truth or, like Bill Clinton, the "technical truth," is done with the intention to deceive, then it's as harmful as any other lie, active or passive.

These "fuzzy around the edges" lies tend to be used most frequently, since little guilt accompanies it. Further, the technical lie is the hardest to spot. But, because you're educating yourself about lying, you'll spot the signs of the technical lie.

Listening for the Signs

When a teenager is trying to work that technical lie, you'll often hear distorted grammar or a misused word. This is known at catachresis—the presence of a misused word should immediately cause your ears to prick up and attend to its context: it's either part of a lie or a lie is soon to follow. You may also hear that the wrong word or syllable is emphasized.

For example, when confronted when stealing from a kiosk in front of a store, the teenager said, "I couldn't have. I didn't even go into the store."

Once, my son, Jack, had a crumb or two of a cookie on his face and shirt. When I asked about the cookie, he answered, "I didn't eat the whole cookie." Another time he answered in that all too familiar passive voice: "The whole cookie was not eaten by me."

Another time, my wife, Debra, questioned our daughter, Camryn, about sneaking a five-dollar-bill from her purse to buy candy. Camryn responded, "I did not have any quarters for the candy machine."

When we grow up, we may hear—or use—the passive voice, too. It's common in business or politics, often expressed in the proverbial phrase, "Mistakes were made." These passive statements avoid using the pronoun, as in, "I (or we) made mistakes," failing to mention who might have been the one to make mistakes. These lies in the passive voice serve a purpose: they allow us to scapegoat government officials and consider them the worst, most morally corrupt of us all. Then we act like our small infractions or breaking of the rules isn't really so bad, because others have done so much worse. I feel good, because anything better than the worst of the worst makes us morally superior. It's a little like the man who has had only one extramarital affair feeling a sense of moral superiority over another who is known to be a chronic womanizer.

Looking Back

When we were kids and heard the story about George Washington admitting that he cut down the cherry tree, we were introduced to the moral ideal: never, never lie. Today, though, this absolute has been replaced by the relative morality of modern public officials, including presidents. Most of us have lived long enough to see many examples of unabashed and unrepentant lying for expedience and personal gain, but at the same time, we often encourage our children to emulate, respect, and adopt these "high officials" as role models of achievement or leadership. (Of course, these individuals sometimes *are* models of these other, more positive traits. They show a mix of behavior and values.)

We carry over from our past this tendency to choose role models among "high officials." However, it's as if we haven't caught up to reality. We actually know much more about individuals in public life today than in the past. In long-gone eras, our presidents were role models we used as examples to teach our children high ideals. But we forget that back then, we knew very little about their private lives or moral lapses. We left it to historians to tell us the truth decades later, if at all. If we had known, we would have faced the same trouble we're in today, because past role models, no matter how we like to venerate them, include people who lied in certain areas of their lives—often their personal lives—that at one time we considered private. If we've learned nothing else from our media-saturated society, it's that lapses in personal behavior don't mean that the public behavior is wrong, too.

Above all, our children are students of cause and effect. They often see that lying leads not to punishment and disgrace, but rather to success and acceptance. So why wouldn't they rapidly learn to adopt and use such behavior in their own lives? How can we expect them not to? Put starkly, they observe and absorb the behavioral adaptation of the amoral, allowing for their survival in the social jungle of our culture.

As If Our Leaders Weren't Bad Enough

Some of our children have a best friend that further promulgates the notion that lying is good. This best friend is always around and is always lying. Sadly, many a child spends most of the waking day outside of school with this friend. Even if a parent is nearby, communication and true interaction is limited when the friend is the focal point.

First, this friend was a loner and went by the name "TV," but now it has a sidekick, "the computer." In the TV medium, the socially approved lie exists in the form of the television commercial or advertisement. We usually warn our kids not to believe what they hear, but the fact remains that our society promotes this mass media lying. Part of basic media literacy involves the knowledge that advertising is meant to persuade and exaggerate the facts or selectively use information to leave positive impressions about products. Within the fair ethics of our capitalist system, persuasion and "cherry picking" shared information are considered okay. Our kids need guidance to understand the motives and goals of advertising, but kids, just like many adults, don't always learn these relatively sophisticated lessons easily.

So we need to acknowledge that modeling starts with us. Our kids experience us lying to them, lying to others—or maybe driving through the toll booth without tossing the exact amount of change into the basket. Then kids are immersed in lying television commercials and, now, web sites that spread lies about all manner of people and situations. In fact, lying on the Internet has become a form of sport for bullies and gossips, not to mention the more malevolent motive to deliberately destroy reputations.

So, like it or not, our children are being inundated with lies, along with the message that lying is good, socially acceptable, and leads to a better life. Lying can even be fun and games. Hence, it is fully understandable that children would lie to their parents without moral compunction or remorse, thus making our job as parental lie detectors even more challenging.

Since I have written and lectured extensively about lying, a producer for Diane Sawyer, of ABC's *Primetime*, approached me to present a program that would help viewers better understand the pervasiveness of childhood lying in our culture today. That's what led to an experiment we conducted in our offices in Chicago that focused on childhood and lying. I'll discuss our findings in the next chapter.

Chapter 2

Childhood Lying—
A Demonstration

A lying adult is easy to spot. During a segment of the television magazine show *Primetime*, Diane Sawyer presented adults lying in three scenarios. The first involved social lying to the opposite sex; in this case, college students meeting for the first time and trying to impress each other. One young man tried to impress a coed by claiming to be the lead musician in a band. The trouble was, he didn't play in a band at all. (A friend of mine told me about the time he tried to impress a woman by claiming to be in law school—but he'd never even gone to college. He was motivated in the moment to lie and worry about the consequences later.) This is very much like George in the TV show, *Seinfeld*, who in various episodes makes false claims about himself, such as being an architect and a marine biologist. His goal is to impress another person, usually a woman.

Another example on *Primetime* presented a classic reason for lying, to avoid punishment. The television crew videotaped cars driving through toll stations without paying, and then the drivers were stopped by the Illinois State Police. When asked why they drove through, the drivers' lies ranged from outright denial ("I paid") to falsifying the circumstances, as in "The coins missed the toll box." Some even said that the drivers' windows had never opened in an attempt to pay. Drivers came up with all sorts of weak excuses—and they were easily shown to be empty words!

A third example of lying involved sparing the feelings of others. The host herself, Diane Sawyer, cooked dinner at her home for the ABC interns, but she'd doctored the chili to taste awful, even nauseating. Unbeknownst to the interns, the dinner party was being secretly videotaped. When asked how they liked the chili, the interns politely lied to Sawyer and complimented her culinary skills. But, after she left the room, the interns became real people again, opening up and talking frankly about how horrible the chili tasted, illustrating their disgust with gag-like gestures.

We've all been in awkward situations where we feel the need to lie. My wife, Debra, and I were dinner guests of a wonderful couple in a suburb of Paris. They had scheduled this feast months in advance and spent weeks preparing for us, and were especially pleased and excited about their goose liver pate. Being vegetarians, but also wanting to be gracious guests, we felt we had to pretend to eat it, furtively stuffing forkfuls in our napkins while praising the hosts. Despite my vegetarian resolve, I let social pressure overwhelm my better judgment, and I ate a few scoops of pate. I spent the next day in bed feeling nauseated with stomach cramps. Obviously, if we had to do it over again, the better choice would have been to risk insulting our guests and apologizing for failing to tell them we didn't eat meat.

Lying in Public

In the late 1990s, I did some research that involved President Bill Clinton and his Grand Jury testimony. It was this work on adult lying that led ABC TV to approach me about investigating lying behavior in children. Oddly enough, while we all know that lying is ubiquitous, we haven't quantified the actual incidence of lying in the population as a whole. Estimates of the incidence of lying within all social interactions range from as low as 25% to as high as 90%. This doesn't give us a very clear picture, and these percentages are probably skewed by variations in what people believe constitutes a lie.

A better way to evaluate the rate of lying focuses on specific situations where lying occurs. For example, lying among college students in a dating situation, as Diane Sawyer demonstrated, has been shown to occur in about 89% of interactions. About 87% of job-hunters will lie on applications and during interviews. We may call it "padding the resumé" or puffing up job descriptions and titles, but it's such a common form of lying that many believe it falls into a so-called "gray area."

Cheating and lying are closely tied, although we haven't accurately measured cheating rates. But a survey of 1,000 high school students found that most tended to believe others were cheating to a significant degree. Those who held this belief were then more likely to admit to incidents of cheating themselves.

One study of cheating behavior investigated college students taking an exam in an introductory psychology course. The study found variation in the cheating rates based on the relative importance of the course to the students. Students who couldn't transfer credits for this course to another school cheated less (53.8%) than students who could transfer credits (65.6%).

A 1998 study suggested a 38% cheating incidence on science tests among sixth, seventh, and eighth grade students. About 36% of college students taking business course exams admitted cheating. The tendency to cheat is a trait that has neither religious nor ethnic boundaries. In a 1996 survey, 70% of high school students at parochial schools admitted to cheating regularly, as did 79% of students in public high schools. Overall, however, most researchers have investigated college students or graduate school students, so we have fewer studies that look at cheating in high school students—the teenagers we're concerned with in this book.

Looking further back into childhood, a 1989 study examined deception in three-year old children. In this study, each child was instructed not to peek at a toy while the experimenter left the room. Of the 33 children tested, 29, or about 88%, "cheated" by peeking at the toy. Among these preschoolers, 38% of those who cheated then lied about it and denied that they had peeked at the toy, and 38% admitted to peeking. The remaining 24% gave no verbal response at all when asked about the toy.

For many of us, the idea of studying deception among three-year-olds might seem a bit odd, and we could certainly argue that at least some of the children did not realize that they were doing anything wrong. But the 38% of the children who peeked and then lied provides some indication of the base rate of lying in very young children.

This study was particularly important because "cheating" was measured though actual observation. Most studies that have investigated cheating have relied upon self-report rather than actual observation—and it seems surprising that when guaranteed anonymity, kids who lie or cheat are willing to admit to it. Studies performed in 1998 of undergraduate cheating suggest rates of 66% or more.

To Lie or Not to Lie . . .

In order to determine the frequency of lying among younger people, I devised an experiment involving 53 students, 16 boys and 37 girls

from grades 1 through 12, which included 28 elementary school students, 16 middle school students, and 9 high school students. We
divided the students into two groups; 26 had no incentive to cheat
or lie, while 27 were given an incentive.

Our students were told that they'd take a spelling test, then be
interviewed about it afterwards, and that at least part of the session
would be videotaped. Then we brought the students into a room and
provided them each with a test and an answer key. We instructed
them not to look at the answer keys until after they had completed
the test. Then they should self-grade the test without changing any
of the answers. We played for the students tape-recorded words
from a spelling book, chosen to be appropriate for their grade level.
Enter the incentives. Half our students were told that anyone who
achieved a score of 100% correct would receive a $10 gift certificate
for a national record store.

After completing the test and self-scoring, I asked the students
if they'd cheated on the test, and, if not, had they been tempted to
do so. Remember, the students were monitored by hidden cameras
throughout the testing.

In addition, the second to the last answer on each word list
answer key was intentionally spelled incorrectly, with a falsely
inserted "y," which served as an additional way to check for cheating. We used two ways to determine the percentage of cheating and
lying. First, I determined the number of students who had incorrectly spelled the intentionally misspelled second to last word on
the answer key. Furthermore, I looked at the videotape for actual
situations of cheating and the number of students who had copied
from the answer key.

So, using the misspelled word as an indicator of cheating, 10
students, or 18.9%, cheated. Of that group, only 3.8% of those with

no incentive offered had cheated, whereas 33% had cheated when provided with the incentive of a "prize" for a perfect score.

However, when we analyzed the videotape, we saw that 39.6% of the students had cheated: 19.2% cheated even when they had no incentive to cheat, while 59.2% cheated when provided an incentive. So we found that even a $10 gift certificate is incentive enough to motivate a substantial majority of students to cheat.

Even more interesting, 21 of the cheating students lied about it, with 19 lying completely, and 2 telling partial lies in which they admitted to copying fewer answers than they'd actually copied.

What does lying about cheating mean? Our results suggest that the students may have felt guilty about cheating, which led to lying about it, or that those inclined to cheat are also inclined to lie. One way or another, cheating easily leads to lying.

We also found that rates of cheating were actually greater in younger children. Among the elementary school students, 38.5% cheated even when there was no incentive to do so, and a full 60% cheated when we provided an incentive. Among junior high students, when no incentive was present, no one cheated. But a whopping 85.7% of those with an incentive cheated on the test. Overall, the mean cheating rates looked like this: 50% for elementary school students, 37.5% for junior high school students, and 22.2% for high school students. So we can see that, regardless of incentive, cheating decreases as kids get into high school.

When we looked at differences in the sexes, we found an even split among elementary school kids, but as the children got older, the cheating rate increased in boys and decreased in girls. By junior high school, only 18.2% of girls cheated, whereas 80% of boys cheated; by high school, 16.7% of girls and 33.3% of boys cheated. These numbers reflect what is reported in real co-educational school settings, although the findings probably underestimate cheating rates because we had a smaller sampling of boys than girls. Had the sample included an equal number of boys and girls then it's likely the rate of overall cheating would have been substantially higher.

The Importance of the Study

This study is so important because cheating was measured by observing actual incidents of cheating, rather than relying on self-reports. Our study also suggested that cheating is prevalent throughout the educational system. It also seems obvious that even a marginal incentive—a $10 gift certificate—caused the cheating rate to jump from about 23% to approximately 60%. So we can extrapolate what this could mean in a classroom setting where performing well or poorly has longer lasting consequences.

I found it particularly surprising that nearly a quarter of the students cheated without the presence of an easily identifiable external incentive. A better grade didn't bring a reward, and no one else would know about their grades on the test. Still, 25% percent cheated anyway. This result gives us reason to question educational programs that offer certificates for entry into theme parks or movie tickets in return for good grades. Tying doing well in school to these types of rewards may have the unintended consequence of encouraging behavior that isn't approved of.

The most striking finding was the 100% concordance between cheating and lying, which may indicate the existence of a separate subgroup of the population who both cheat and lie. Looking at these individuals in an adult population, we could speculate that they may fit the characteristics of a sociopathic personality disorder, that is, those who have no moral barrier to lying. These individuals may also be physically aggressive or show mentally dominating behavior.

Based on current statistics, the incidence of sociopathic behavior in the general population is approximately 1 to 3%, which is much lower than the 60% incidence of cheating and lying found in my study. So it's unlikely that the presence of sociopathic personality disorders explain cheating in children. Our kids are not criminal sociopaths, but rather, they are normal children. Like it or not, normal children lie, even with the slightest of incentives. When it comes to covering up some kind of mistake or deliberate wrongdoing, we're on solid ground when we say that all kids lie. If a teenage George Washington had chopped down the cherry tree, my study suggests that he would not have admitted to it! He would have sworn up and down and sideways that he'd hadn't been anywhere in the vicinity of that tree. Or he'd have resorted to the passive voice: "The tree was not near me."

Why Do Normal Children Lie?

It isn't clear why children lie in general or lie about cheating in particular. Perhaps they fear loss of self-esteem if they do poorly. Or maybe they believe they can get away with lying, which makes it okay. Maybe they fear paying a penalty for failing. Or we could flip those motivations around. Maybe they lie not to preserve self-esteem, but to enhance it. Maybe they feel good about getting away with something. Maybe they deny cheating, not just to the examiner (in this case, me), but they deny cheating even to themselves. Covering up cheating is then justified.

Lying to oneself is hardly uncommon—we see it over and over again among adults as well as children. Humans tend to be narcissistic and believe we are good. We can tell ourselves we are good at the same time we're actually doing something bad. Therefore, we didn't do a bad thing, or if something bad happened, someone else must have done it.

When confronted with the reality of cheating, just two students admitted cheating and then, only on some answers. In other words, they minimized what they'd done. They also expressed the belief that their behavior wasn't "really cheating," because they thought they knew the answer in their head before copying it down from the answer key. This denial provides an out. It allows cheaters to rationalize that they have not really cheated (presumably because they really knew the answer); therefore, they eliminate any guilt over cheating. Hence, we see a slippery definition of cheating, in this case based on situational convenience. If children (and adults) believe they didn't cheat, then lying becomes easier. In this convoluted thinking, to deny cheating, that isn't really cheating, is no longer a lie.

While our sample size was small, we saw that the rates of cheating dropped quite significantly (down to 20%) by high school. Yet, other research indicates the rate rises again among college students. Perhaps socialization against cheating during the pre-college years makes the difference, or it's possible that those accepted into college are among those who are prone to cheating, a kind of selection bias. It could also be a result of increased incentive to cheat in college and graduate school, where pressure to do well intensifies—and certainly exceeds the value of a $10 gift certificate.

My study included a small sample from a Midwestern metropolitan population. It's possible that a larger sample from varying geographic locations would have led to different results. Furthermore, with a larger sample size, we could have found differences in subgroups, that is, age, sex, and ethnic or racial differences. However, to my knowledge, this is the first study to directly observe cheating during an activity that simulated a realistic school situation.

Our intentionally misspelled answer key word, as an indicator of cheating, grossly underestimated cheating when surreptitiously observed; 18.9% cheated on the spelling of that word, versus 39.6% on the test as a whole, as observed on the secret video-tape. How do we explain this disparity? One possibility is that the children were familiar enough with the misspelled word to know that the answer key was incorrect. In fact, one child stated, "The answer key has a spelling error." If this was the case, participants who were cheating would ignore the misspelled word on the answer key, and spell it correctly.

A second possibility is that, when cheating, participants made errors such that they incorrectly copied the answers from the answer key. This was seen on surreptitious observation. Occasionally students would incorrectly copy the answer key and then, on self-grading, would grade the answer correct, even though it was incorrectly spelled on the test sheet and did not match the answer sheet. Part of the incidence of this miscopying an intentionally false word may be due to dyslexia, and part may be due to simple carelessness.

What Does This Mean for All of Us?

The implications of cheating are grave. Since school is the work of children, and cheating and lying are prevalent in this group, what happens when children become adults and spend most of their waking hours at work? If cheating and lying on spelling tests are viewed as morally acceptable, then under what circumstances are cheating and lying unacceptable? Is cheating okay on a science test or a job interview? Or, to use a dramatic example, is cheating okay during surgery or when trying a murder case?

Clearly, although President Clinton didn't invent lying and cheating, his and others' public behavior may have opened the door to further disintegration of this moral concept, especially among the younger generation. In general, those in the media and other public figures showed a degree of passive acceptance of the Commander in Chief's behavior. Most of the public preferred not to have his private behavior lead to political consequences.

While that slightly ho-hum stance might be a sign of sophistication on the part of adults, our kids may have seen it as a willingness to relax morals when it comes to cheating and lying behaviors. After all, if it's okay for the President to lie, why isn't a teenager also entitled to tell a few convenient lies?

While it's true that today's teens probably don't have clear memories of President Clinton's scandal, at the time, teens became part of the conversation about personal behavior among public figures. Like athletes and actors, politicians whose scandals grab public attention are in part evaluated by the kinds of behavior they model to the rest of us, especially our children.

All public individuals, and that includes celebrities, athletes, and most certainly presidents and others in high positions, are role models today, whether we like it or not, and the scrutinizing of a public figure intensifies when his or her behavior is rumored to be particularly outrageous or actually illegal.

It's possible that this willingness to lie is relative, in that kids and adults may claim moral high ground in all other ways than this one lie—whatever that lie happens to be. Regardless of the nuances, our study demonstrated that lying, and its cousin, cheating, often occur spontaneously without particular incentive and can be easily generated with the slightest incentive. So, just think of all the expensive material things that your teenager wants, from a Game

Boy® to a Playstation® to iPhone®. As you can see, the temptation to lie is enormous, and even in the best among them, the temptation for teenagers to lie—and the prevalence of the behavior—is overwhelming.

Chapter 3

Nature's Lies

I'm going to take a detour to add some perspective about deception and lies that we rarely, if ever, link to human behavior, and by the same token, some human behavior that we would never label deception that actually is. First, we are born to lie—it's part of what keeps the species going. When some behavior occurs over and over in human endeavors, we tend to view it as natural, beneficial behavior in some way. In fact, the males that lie most successfully are able to dominate and establish an edge in mating.

What this means in evolutionary terms is a selective advantage among those who are the most successful liars. That's what we mean when we say that it's in our nature to lie, and the drive to lie has applied to all societies throughout human history, regardless of other cultural traits. It even exists among other, more primitive species. Amongst the great apes and gorillas, for example, Jane Goodall and Diane Fosse both observed behaviors which anthropomorphically can be described as intentional deception, or lying. This deception involves exaggerating physical attributes, which provides them greater status. By deceiving other members of his community or

band, a great ape or gorilla is able to obtain more food and intimi-
date the challenging males in order to maintain dominance. This in
turn enhances his survival and chance for procreation and genetic
predominance. Nature's intent is to promote the survival of the fit-
test in whatever form that takes.

Since lying is a cross-cultural phenomenon, we see it as a theme
in our myths, religions, and literature. Just look at the Adam and Eve
story: One bite of the apple means a fall from grace for all humanity
and no more paradise, no more Garden of Eden. When Eve succumbs to temptation and then lies about eating from the Tree of
Knowledge of Good and Evil, it sets out the premise for what many
religions call sin. Virtually all religions have a prohibition against
lying. In fact, it is these elaborate rules governing truth and untruth
that testify to the existence and regular occurrence of lying. If it
didn't run rampant, there'd be no reason to create rules against it.

Fast forward to Harry Potter's Hogwarts School, and we see the
themes of lying and its consequences run through the story. Harry
and his friends are affected by lies others tell them, but they're also
affected by the lies they tell to protect themselves. These students
never know at the beginning of each adventure who is good and
who is evil. Part of using their wits to survive and protect each other
and the school involves assessing the honesty of others and lying
when they think they've identified deceptive behavior in those
who threaten harm. Of course, wizardry and all ancient and modern magic involve lying in the form of omission and secrecy—and
things are never what they seem.

Nature's Deception

If you want to talk to your children about the concept of deception,
then nature provides plenty of examples to use. For example, all kids

are fascinated by chameleons, animals endowed with the lying trait. Chameleons change the appearance of their skin to background colors to provide camouflage. This is a form of deception, a lie communicated to potential predators. In another example, female emperor penguins deceive their mates into thinking they fathered their eggs. The male penguin diligently cares for the eggs of his mate, but he may not be the one that fertilized those eggs. As a result, the "duped" male spends time and effort protecting the egg until it hatches, mistakenly assuming he is the father. In two more examples, butterflies with images that look like eyes on their wings deceive other insects about their size, and the praying mantis adopts a stick-like appearance to deceive potential predators.

You can also point out nature's mechanism for deception among the non-animal kingdom. The Venus Flytrap lures the fly with a sticky and odoriferous substance. (Not only flies are fooled by this aroma. My family's dog, Cosette, sniffed out and devoured the Venus Flytrap we had just purchased for our son Jack's science project.) Even a beckoning flower tricks the bee into its sweet petals to furtively induce pollination. While both benefit from this arrangement, it's as if mutual benefit comes from mutual lying. The bee is lured by the nectar of the petals, and it's the flower's intention to suffuse the bee with pollen. In this system, the bee is lured by one thing in order to accomplish another of nature's goals. Regardless of the beneficial nature of the outcome, nature still arranges this exchange as a kind of trick.

Beyond Instinct to Choice

While it's fun to talk to kids about nature's deceptions, they soon understand the difference between involuntary behavior in nature and free will. No animal even comes close to creating the elaborate web of lies that humans are capable of, and animals don't have the capacity for guilt. Most of us don't experience guilt when we altruistically lie. Sociopathic liars don't feel guilt either, because they lack the capacity for it. But in virtually all other situations, lying results in guilt, because the knowledge of right and wrong, of ethical imperative, separates us from the rest of the animal kingdom.

Birds and apes may use tools, and some species of monkeys have been taught to use a sign language and teach it to other monkeys. The dolphin has a brain larger than a human's. So what separates our evolutionary path from that of other species? It comes down to opposable thumbs and our capacity for a moral code. Sure, maybe someday we will discover a sloth or some such creature with an opposable thumb, but I'd rather be distinguished as a species with a moral code than for our flexible digits.

We call our deceptions lies because we set up a code that demonstrates that we "know better." When your eight-year-old comes to you complaining that her three-year-old brother ruined her toy, we try to explain it and ease her anger by saying that "he didn't know any better." And that's the way we begin to teach and reinforce the code that we expect the child to learn. Puppies who chew shoes don't know any better, but adults who steal the shoes do—or should.

The Need to Lie

At the same time we teach children a moral code, we also show them circumstances when, apparently, it is okay to lie and deceive. We have developed elaborate games, like poker, as outlets to harmlessly channel our urges to lie. A person with a "poker face" is generally admired for the ability to withhold the truth.

In games and in life, we lie to others, but more often we lie to ourselves. In some respects we are all "mythomaniacs," meaning that in a few areas we're like pathological liars, who believe their own lies. We have the ability to proceed through life engrossed in our pedestrian concerns, not only repressing the certainty of our mortality, but deceiving ourselves about immortality. In Western societies we're taught (for the most part) Judeo-Christian concepts of an afterlife, of heaven and hell. Yet, even with reward or punishment at the end of the line, we are on an almost unending quest for material things and a good time at any cost. Our materialism and hedonism usually trump piety! So, belief in a higher power aside, we live the big lie until illness thrusts the myth of immortality from our grasps. Based on Elizabeth Kubler-Ross's research about attitudes toward death and dying, most of us try to deny and bargain with this higher power in order to maintain our self-deception of immortality for just a little longer. We see this drive to hang on to our self-deception even among those in the last stages of dying.

Philosophers and others will argue that self-deception is necessary to survive and thrive. After all, if we spent our days focused on the fact that we're dying, we wouldn't set goals or dream and plan for the future. We might not paint masterpieces or build castles or compose music or study philosophy. Ironically, lying, in the form of self-deception about our mortality, has allowed our societies to flourish and our species to survive.

Working with or against Our Nature

Bringing the discussion closer to home, we're forced to grapple with our kids over lying. Just because lying is a part of human nature and has helped us survive as a species doesn't mean it's a beneficial characteristic in our advanced societies.

All kinds of actions may have helped primitive humans survive, but as we developed into societies, we adopted the "Ten Commandments" solution to civilize us and establish a moral code. Hence, our religions and customs and even laws prohibit lying, stealing, and killing. The law about these things vary, but every society has rules that govern these areas of life, and we use shared, public resources to enforce these rules.

If our concerns were strictly self-preservation, we'd encourage aggressive, dominating behavior, even stealing or killing to create advantage. But those behaviors break down societies—the many instances of genocide we've seen in the twentieth and the current century stand as depressing examples of what happens when certain behaviors become tolerated.

Similarly, lying destroys the trust required for social interaction and a functioning society. Without trust, people could not group together, and life, as we know it, would no longer exist. We would be a "society of the shark," in which the only commandments are strength, power, and self-survival. But, as we know, all cultures allow prohibited behavior as long as it's strictly regulated. We allow—encourage—killing in war as long as we follow the "rules," and we can use lethal injections or gas chambers to kill those we label murderers. Of course, we can become spies and lie and kill for a living while serving our country.

Presenting False Images

A more universal, socially accepted, and subtle form of lying involves the way we present ourselves. Like the ancient Greek actors whose faces were covered in masks, we try to project to others our idealized image of ourselves, or in other words, we try to present ourselves as better (by the accepted standards) than we truly are. Despite the adage that perfection (or success) is a journey, not a destination, we all want to be viewed as if we have reached that destination.

On a physical level, women, and some men, color their hair and wear makeup to look younger and less rocked by time or by the vicissitudes of life, including illness. That accounts for the meteoric rise in popularity of Botox® and other cosmetic procedures, including face lifts.

Since advances in medicine and public health have allowed the ranks of the elderly to swell, we see even greater attempts to deceive others about our ages. At one time, a tiny percentage of the U.S. population had reached age 65, but today almost 13% of the population is over age 65, and by 2020 a full 20% of the population will be over 65 years old. Despite this trend, we still idealize youth, which drives the desire to look young. This discrepancy between actual and desired age often generates anxiety and lack of self-worth.

So today we see that some among the elderly lie to themselves about their ages. They do things generally associated with youth in an attempt to deny to themselves that they are aging. However, in order to deny aging, they may also cheat themselves from using the wisdom that they've worked hard over the years to gain.

The term "aging gracefully" embodies the idea of a psychological state of wisdom and certainly working to stay in good health. In our society, good health equals youth, so engaging in regular exercise, for example, is part of maintaining youthfulness. On the one hand, it is uplifting to see older people running marathons or hiking the Rockies. It shows the reality that aging doesn't mean pulling up a rocking chair and sitting on the sidelines until we die.

On the other hand, certain actions, usually those that lack wisdom, may promote self-denial and acceptance of the inevitably advancing years. We usually see this in age-defying actions like bungee-jumping, or in frivolous things like buying an expensive sports car or a jazzy motorcycle. Sometimes the actions, such as sexual pro-miscuity, can enter into dangerous territory.

Many older people will do almost anything—relatively benign things—to avoid the outward signs of aging. They'll wear contact lenses and hidden hearing aids, and try to avoid using canes. (Sometimes the spouses of those using canes don't like them either—it's "age by association.") Both men and women may dress in clothing designed for people half their age. In other words, we train the elderly to try to deceive, the same way we train kids to hide their cards when we're teaching them card games. We encourage socially acceptable deception.

Even the nose gets into the act and has the power to aid in "age deception." We've known for many years that adding odors to the environment can alter both behavior and perceptions. For example, in the presence of an added scent, gamblers will spend more time at a particular slot machine. The presence of some odors influences the perception of size or age. When we studied this, we found that when a woman wore the aroma of pink grapefruit, men perceived them as being six years younger—we could call that a form of olfactory Botox®. It's like sniffing through rose-colored glasses, and it's also a subtle form of lying used to change perceptions.

In an analogous fashion, we've found that the "scent environment" can affect weight perception. We tested the effect of odors on men's perception of a model's weight, and when a woman wore a mixed floral spicy aroma, men perceived them to be approximately 12 pounds lighter. Another example of "deception" through the senses!

I mention these things, not to say that coloring our hair or getting Botox® treatments or wearing spicy colognes is an example of true lying, but rather to illustrate the nuances of deception. We could debate about the wisdom of a society treating age or being overweight as conditions to hide or camouflage, but that kind of lying doesn't rise to the kind of moral standards that we must uphold when we raise children to tell the truth.

Sometimes we're handed the opportunity to study known lying, and a former U.S. president offered just that.

Chapter 4

Become a Human Lie Detector: What I Learned from President Bill Clinton

He that has eyes to see and ears to hear may convince himself
that no mortal can keep a secret. If his lips are silent, he chatters
with his fingertips: betrayal oozes out of him at every pore
—Sigmund Freud

About twenty years ago, a survey found that 90% of Americans admitted to lying regularly. This survey was taken before the public scandal involving former President Bill Clinton, although political scandals were—and are—nothing new. Scandals arising from those in power in government go back to the beginning of the U.S.— witness the duel between Aaron Burr and Alexander Hamilton or Thomas Jefferson, who it appears was the father of more than just the Constitution. Each recent decade has brought its own set of scandals, often involving money and power and, of course, the occasional sexual peccadillo. However in the 1990s, our overall ethics and morality as a society were relatively unchallenged, and, in a way, we adopted a "ho-hum" attitude about a range of scandals, as in, "What can we expect? This is what people in power do."

Most of us have a remarkably high tolerance for lying on many levels, and this spills over into daily lives, seen in a casual attitude toward honesty and truthfulness. We may see evidence of this informal attitude in our own offices and homes, but it ripples through all of our institutions. For example, doctors often encounter lying in the form of malingering, which is feigning or faking illness. Neurologic disorders such as low-back pain, neck pain, and headaches are among the most commonly feigned illnesses.

At the same time, accurately assessing the tendency to lie is difficult at best. In forensic psychiatry, mental health professionals routinely examine a subject's history in order to establish what is true and what is false. They also weigh signs of both candor and disingenuousness during physical examinations. I once examined a prisoner who described total amnesia on the day his wife was repeatedly stabbed to death, yet he had full and accurate recall of the day before and the day after the murder. His neurologic examination was totally normal, too, and this suggests that he showed a form of malingering, in this case, feigned amnesia.

Another example of disingenuous behavior occurred when I was called by the Illinois State Attorney General's office to evaluate a prisoner on death row. He had been scheduled for execution later in the week, and a temporary stay of execution had been ordered after his attorneys questioned his mental status—was he mentally competent to be executed? (This is one of the oddities of our system, in that we sometimes treat death row prisoners to make sure they're mentally and physically healthy enough to be aware that they're being executed.) In this particular case, a prestigious neurologist from a university hospital had examined him and found him to be mentally incompetent, with an inability to understand or even speak. As a result, a petition was submitted to the court suggesting that execution of such a mentally incompetent individual would be cruel and unusual punishment. The state's attorney requested that I evaluate the prisoner to determine his neurologic status and whether he was truly mentally incompetent.

I arrived at the jail with some degree of trepidation. While I have examined many criminals in the past, I had never examined a person on death row. I tried to be particularly careful, bringing all my tools of examination—reflex hammer, pin wheel, eye chart, tongue blade, penlight, and the like—with the realization that any of them could be used as a weapon against me if the prisoner were able to get hold of them. This man had nothing to lose—he was already scheduled to be executed within the week. He had been informed that I was there to examine him in order for the execution to be carried out.

I spent several hours with him. When I first arrived, he was mute and uncommunicative. Over time, as I sat and talked with him, he began to move his lips as if he were able to answer questions, and as I continued, he began to actually whisper words to me, which were clearly in response to my questions. He was able to answer appropriately all questions about his name, age, location, and other pertinent demographic information, but he demonstrated evidence of Ganser's syndrome.

Ganser's syndrome is a phenomenon of approximate answers. It's seen in prisoners, in military recruits who do not want to continue serving in the military, and in other people in similar situations. Individuals with this syndrome will be able to answer questions, but the answers will always be somewhat incorrect, even for the simplest of questions. So, for instance, when I asked the prisoner what two plus two equaled, he responded, "Three." When asked about the color of the sky he said, "yellow." When I asked him to point out north on a compass, he pointed downwards. When asked to spell the word "world," he spelled, "w-o-d-r-l." Asked about the date, he gave the exact day and month, but the year was off by a decade.

Despite this, when I tested his ability to recall objects, he displayed a normal ability, and when I asked him to recall parts of the examination, he was perfectly normal. All the remainder of his examination was normal. At the beginning of the examination I gave him four objects to remember, and at the end of the examination he reminded me that I had not asked him what those four objects were. In speaking with the guard during a short break, the guard told me that at night the prisoner would play chess by calling out moves to a prisoner in a cell across from him, using standard International Chess Federation nomenclature.

All this from an individual who, just the day before, a neurologist had suggested, was so mentally disabled that he was not even able to speak or understand rudimentary language. Based on my examination, I reported to the court that the prisoner was mentally competent and was indeed malingering—pretending—to be mentally incompetent when in actuality he had his wits about him, so to speak.

As my findings were about to be formally presented in court, the attorneys in charge of this prisoner's appeals produced a videotape of a confession by someone else to the crime for which this prisoner had been convicted. The prisoner was let go, and, upon his release, he addressed the press—in perfect diction—and thanked his supporters for helping him during his false imprisonment. So, while this man showed us a good example of malingering, it was done for survival, in order to overcome an injustice, and his case was covered by the national media because it indeed was a close call. Given what was going on behind the scenes to expose the real murderer, the prisoner and his lawyers had just needed to keep buying more time.

"Lying" on his examination and to physicians was understandable, and he was indeed able to fool the prisoner's first neurologist.

Sometimes individuals lie, or malinger, for economic gain. At the request of an attorney, I saw a woman in Texas who claimed to have been exposed to hydrogen sulfide, a toxic chemical that at low concentrations smells like rotten eggs, but at high concentrations anesthetizes the olfactory nerve and thus becomes odorless. This occurred during an accident at the chemical plant next door to her house. This incident allegedly caused problems with her memory, logical thinking, cognition, and emotions, and she claimed her life was ruined. She lost her sex drive and divorced. Her inability and unwillingness to socialize with other people left her isolated at home, where her life wasn't much better since she couldn't concentrate long enough to watch a television commercial, must less read a book.

In obtaining her history and examination, I found multiple discrepancies between her complaints and her physical findings. For example, when we test memory, one of the tell tale signs of false memory loss is when one is able to recall more digits when repeated backwards than when repeated forwards. As part of the mental state examination, when asking a patient to recall numbers, the examining neurologist or psychiatrist will say the numbers, one per second, in a random order, and ask the patient to recall and repeat them. Until the advent of cell phones, most people memorized a handful of regularly called phone numbers. Several studies of memory established that a normal person can recall the same number of digits as a phone number, seven digits, forwards and four to five digits backwards. In someone who does not have true organic memory loss, but rather, is pretending to have memory loss, the number of digits that they recall backwards will exceed the number that they recall forwards. This woman was only able to recall two numbers forwards, but seven numbers backwards, even greater than the number I'd expect to see in a totally normal college professor, suggesting not impaired, but rather enhanced cognitive ability.

In addition, she was unable to do virtually anything on the examination. When asked to name the current president, she said she thought it was John F. Kennedy. She claimed not to be able to spell simple words correctly or even correctly write her name. When asked to raise her right hand, she raised her left foot. When asked to raise her left foot, she raised her right hand. When asked to walk in a normal manner she displayed what is called astasia-abasia, that is, wildly dramatic movements and moving from side to side without falling. (For those old enough to remember, this is reminiscent of the "Teaberry shuffle" seen in commercials in the 1970s, in which an old woman would jump around the room in response to the taste of gum, or how the old man, Mr. Six, danced around in television commercials for Six Flags Amusement Park.)

My patient was able to move around in apparent precarious positions without falling—she displayed ballet-like ability to walk. Despite this, she entered the examination room barely able to stand, requiring two people to assist her onto the examination table. However, when she asked to use the restroom, she was wheeled to the washroom. When she was between the hall and the washroom and assumed she wasn't being observed, we surreptitiously video-taped her easily standing on her own and rapidly walking, almost running, to the ladies' room.

As part of her assessment, we obtained a twenty-four-hour urine collection to evaluate metabolites of norepinephrine, which would help us detect a chemical imbalance in the brain. She took the collection bottle to the hotel where she was staying and brought the specimen back the next morning. To fully understand what she did next, I must tell you that in front of our office is a loading point for horse-drawn buggies that take tourists on scenic rides around down-town Chicago. When her urine analysis arrived from the laboratory a week later, results were positive for horse urine!

What we have here is a clear example of an individual attempting to malinger, or fake illness, for potential monetary gain. Upon her findings, I notified her legal counsel, who thanked me very much, but asked that I not send a report. This was the last I ever heard from that attorney.

The Surprising Truth about Uncovering a Lie

I just presented two situations in which I was successful at identifying malingering. Unfortunately, however, physicians in general are not very good at identifying lying and deception. Upon formal assessment, psychiatrists are only 57% accurate in recognizing deception, not much better than flipping a coin. Moreover, they don't have much insight that their own lie-detecting abilities are poor, but actually claim confidence that is inversely proportional to their accuracy. So, in any given situation, the more certain they are about not being fooled, the more likely they are to have been deceived!

When it comes to lying, certain principles apply. One involves the intensity of the liar's belief. The more the liar believes in the lie, the more difficult it is to detect the truth. This makes sense because successful liars, first of all, deceive themselves. With complete self-deception, liars are "undetectable."

In addition, the consultation-liaison process in our current healthcare system and the bureaucracy in the educational system actually makes it easier for the liar. The more often the liar repeats the lie, the harder it is to be detected, and the more believable it becomes. For the liar, "practice makes perfect," and the medical and educational hierarchies enable liars to rehearse their histories. For example, by the time a prevaricator sees a psychiatrist, he may have already repeated his lies to a multitude of physicians, residents, and medical students, giving him opportunities to improve his deceptive presentation. Similarly, by the time your child expresses his lie to you, he's already told the teacher, principal, and possibly the police. This sort of repetition and practice converts him into a skilled fabulist, or liar, with his lying skills honed to perfection with each repetition.

The "Pinocchio Effect" Is Born

As a psychiatrist, I can say that lying was not at the top of my investigative agenda. Besides, like my colleagues, I thought I was good at detecting deception and that ultimately, the lie would come out.

During much of my professional life, I've been immersed in studying the sense of smell, specifically odors and their effects on behavior. For instance, we found that tastants called Sensa, when sprinkled on food, facilitated weight loss. (See appendix for more information.) One area I've studied and about which I have written several articles and a book, *Scentsational Sex*, focuses on the effects of odors on sexual arousal. When one is sexually aroused, there occurs engorgement of the erectile tissue in the nose—and yes, there is erectile tissue in the nose. As this tissue becomes engorged, breathing through the nose becomes more difficult, and that offers an explanation why people pant when sexually aroused.

With nasal engorgement, eddy currents develop inside the nose as a person inhales. These are like internal nasal tornadoes, and they cause odor molecules to be diverted up to the olfactory epithelium—the lining—at the top of the nose, rather than following the normal path down the bronchi into the lungs. This diversion of the air currents means that sexual arousal results in increased ability to smell.

Since everything in nature has a purpose, this olfactory diversion may be the body's attempt to achieve the greatest chance of recognizing pheromones (invisible chemical messengers thought to be involved with attraction and arousal) and, in turn, to increase the chance of successful procreation.

This observation about nasal engorgement with sexual arousal led me to wonder what else might cause the same nasal engorgement, and that train of thought led me to think about lying. When we lie, we usually feel guilty. This guilty emotion leads to a sympathetic nervous system discharge, a flight-or-fight response, which triggers an increase in the release of adrenaline into the blood. When this occurs, we see an increase in blood pressure and heart rate. A lie detector can measure these changes.

The elevated blood pressure then causes an increase in blood flow to the erectile tissues in the body, including the erectile tissues in the nose, which induces an internal nasal expansion or swelling. As a result, changes in a particular kind of white blood cell, the mast cell, occur, and histamine is released, which induces the nose to begin to itch. In response to this sensation, the prevaricator scratches the nose. It's folk wisdom that telling a lie will make one's nose grow. So, I named this nasal engorgement and the nose-scratching associated with lying "the Pinocchio Effect."

Although I'd written a few articles about this phenomenon, I had moved on to other studies. However, in September of 1998, I was working out on an exercise bicycle while watching the videotape of President Bill Clinton testifying before the grand jury on a nearby TV set. When I say watching, I mean that literally because I didn't have headphones on, so I couldn't hear the voices. However, I watched the President repeatedly touching his nose and had an epiphany. Without knowing what he was saying, I knew he was clearly lying, and I wondered if anyone else knew it as surely as I did.

The Nose Really Knows

Intrigued by this tape, a medical student (at the time), Charles Wolff, from the University of Illinois (now at Baylor Medical College), and I performed a formal analysis. We compared 12 minutes of grand jury investigation tape (released to the public just over four weeks after President Clinton's August 17, 1998, testimony), during which President Clinton denied having a sexual relationship with former White House intern Monica Lewinski, with two other tapes on which it was known that he had spoken truthfully. On the tape containing the untruthful grand jury testimony, he touched his nose 0.26 times per minute, whereas during the tapes in which he was truthful, he did not touch his nose at all.

I thought this was uncannily revealing and went back over the psychiatric literature. We looked at 54 peer-reviewed articles and 20 books on truthfulness and lying, and from these sources, we selected 23 practical, objective signs a psychiatrist, or parent for that matter, could use as evidence of dishonesty and deception. Of these 23 signs of lying, President Clinton markedly displayed 21 during his testimony.

Signs of lying included use of the following:

Qualifiers/modifiers: Examples include "not necessarily," "but," "however," "ordinarily," "almost," "most of the time," generally," "essentially," "basically," "sometimes," "usually," "hardly ever," "possibly," "actually, "rarely," "specifically," "some."

Expanded contractions: Liars tend to emphasize the "not" to declare that they were not involved. They use the expanded form of a verb more frequently than the contraction. Examples: "did not" versus "didn't," or "could not" versus "couldn't," and "would not" versus "wouldn't."

Denials of lying: The liar denies lying and emphasizes the truthfulness of his answers. For example: "I have absolutely no reason to lie," "frankly," "obviously," "to be one hundred percent honest," "to tell the truth," "I am being straightforward," "believe me," "honestly," "to the best of my knowledge," "as far as I know."

Errors in speech: These might include changes of thought in mid-sentence, grammatical errors including tense, person, and pronoun, and Freudian slips.

Pause fillers: These are non-word sounds used to fill in time during a period of hesitation, such as "uh," "er," "um," and "ah."

Stuttering: The liar becomes tongue-tied, slurs his speech, stammers, and stutters.

Throat clearing: Liars will clear their throat and make other sounds such as moaning, groaning, or grunting.

Avoidance of pointing: The liar tends to avoid pointing or raising a single finger to illustrate a point.

A liar's postural shifts: Coincident with lying, the liar leans forward, resting elbows on knees or a table, and constantly changes
posture or position in the chair.

**Licking and puckering and
tightening the lips:** The liar
frequently uses the tongue to
lick the lips and tighten the
mouth, as if preventing anything from getting out.

Drinking and swallowing: The liars will take more sips from a water bottle or glass nearby and swallow more often than someone telling the truth.

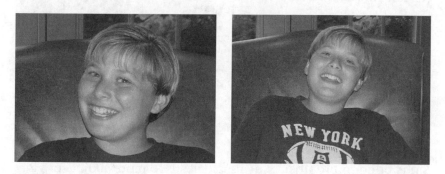

Smiling and laughing: When lying, the person will smile more—insincere smiles—and laugh inappropriately.

Fewer hand gestures: Truthful persons often use wide, sweeping hand gestures while talking or illustrating a point. Liars use fewer hand gestures.

Hand-to-face grooming (excluding nose): Someone lying will show increased touching of the face, ears, or hair.

Sighs or deep breaths: Lying usually leads to more audible or visible sighs or deep breaths.

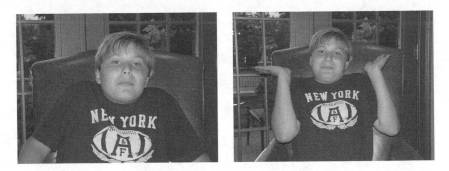

Hand and shoulder shrugs: The liar will flip the hands over in an open fashion and shrug the shoulders as if uncertain.

Handling objects: This looks like nervous fidgeting, and the dishonest person will be more than typically preoccupied with such objects as eyeglasses, pen, or papers.

Averting gaze: Looking away to the side, or down, after having made eye contact is usually a sign of deception.

Less blinking: A deceptive person blinks less often.

Crossing arms: Folding or crossing the arms creates a barrier against the one being lied to.

Closing hands and interlocking fingers: Either hand is closed into a fist, with no fingers shown, or the two hands have their fingers interlocked.

Touching nose: Scratching, rubbing, or touching the nose is a sign of the nasal engorgement that results from lying.

Constructing the "Pinocchio" Study

Dr. Wolff and I examined a 23–minute segment of a videotape and the verbatim transcript of President Clinton's testimony before a federal grand jury taken on that date in August 1998, parts of which have subsequently been determined to be false, including his denial that he had a sexual relationship with Monica Lewinsky. We determined the frequency of the 23 signs indicative of lying that appear in this segment.

We also examined two other videotapes and transcripts of speech segments. The first was 11 minutes of the same grand jury testimony in which he answered basic questions—for example, his name and his attorneys' names. This functioned as the internal control, that is, a segment within the same tape that we could consider the baseline for truthfulness. The second was five minutes of a fund-raising speech to a sympathetic crowd on behalf of a political candidate in Chicago on September 25, 1998. That was the external control.

We measured the frequency of each the 23 signs in these three segments by rate per minute, and then compared and analyzed the data for statistical significance of the difference. The signs of deception were markedly more frequent during the dishonest segment than during either of the two honest segments.

Tables 1 and 2 show the frequency with which each of the signs occurred in the mendacious speech compared with their frequency in the external and internal periods.

We examined the grand jury testimony tape to confirm what was later revealed. Despite one's opinion about Bill Clinton, his presidency, and the justification for pursuing his impeachment, the signs of deceptive speech are apparent. And I'm using this example because this video testimony is infamous and virtually everyone in the country had access to it. You can bet many teenagers also watched it. (And, like many of their elders, probably snickered over it, too.)

Table 1   **Frequency of Signs Indicative of Deception in the Mendacious Speech Versus the External Control**

	Times Per Minute		
	External Control	Mendacious Speech	% of Change
Verbal signs			
Qualifies and modifiers	1.4	2.26	+61
Expanded contractions	0.2	0.39	+95
Denials of lying	0.0	1.34	>100
Speech errors	0.4	1.65	+313
Pause fillers	1.0	1.78	+78
Stuttering	0.4	1.39	+248
Throat clearing	0.0	0.74	>100
Nonverbal signs			
Less finger pointing	1.6	0.52	-52
Lean or postural shift	0.0	0.87	>100
Lip licking	1.4	1.40	No change
Lip tightening	0.4	0.43	+7.5
Drinking and swallowing	0.2	0.91	+355
Smiling	0.8	0.52	-35*
Fewer hand gestures	7.8	3.40	-56
Hand to face	0.2	0.70	+250
Sighs	0.0	0.22	>100
Shrugs	0.0	0.22	>100
Handling objects	0.0	0.57	>100
Averting gaze	1.2	3.83	+219
Less blinking	11.8	43.40	+268*
Crossing arms	0.0	0.04	>100
Closing hands	0.6	1.90	+217
Touching nose	0.0	0.26	>100

* The changed frequency of the sign is not in the direction suggestive of deception.

Table 2 **Frequency of Signs Indicative of Deception in the Mendacious Speech Versus the Internal Control**

	Times Per Minute		
	External Control	Mendacious Speech	% of Change
Verbal signs			
Qualifies and modifiers	0.45	2.26	+402
Expanded contractions	0.18	0.39	+117
Denials of lying	0.82	1.34	+63
Speech errors	0.09	1.65	+1733
Pause fillers	0.55	1.78	+224
Stuttering	0.09	1.39	+1444
Throat clearing	0.18	0.74	+311
Nonverbal signs			
Less finger pointing	0.00	0.52	>100*
Lean or postural shift	0.18	0.87	+383
Lip licking	0.91	1.40	+54
Lip tightening	0.55	0.43	-22*
Drinking and swallowing	0.64	0.91	+42
Smiling	0.27	0.52	+93
Fewer hand gestures	0.36	1.40	+844*
Hand to face	0.09	0.70	+678
Sighs	0.36	0.22	-39*
Shrugs	0.18	0.22	+22
Handling objects	0.27	0.57	+111
Averting gaze	2.91	3.83	+32
Less blinking	50.50	43.4	-14
Crossing arms	0.00	0.04	>100
Closing hands	0.64	1.90	+197
Touching nose	0.00	0.26	>100

* The changed frequency of the sign is not in the direction suggestive of deception.

Certain signs of lying were particularly noteworthy, including denials of lying, throat clearing, leaning forward, sighs, shrugs, handling objects, crossing arms, and touching the nose (Table 1). Two of these signs were also absent from the internal control: crossing arms and touching the nose (Table 2).

The difference in the signs is more marked when we compared his testimony to the political rally setting, when he'd presumably be far less anxious. But we could also see substantial difference when the president was answering non-threatening questions before the grand jury. The differences were marked in many ways. President Clinton showed 20 of 23 signs during the part of the grand jury testimony that was later determined to be false. Taken individually, only two signs met the criterion for statistical significance: fewer hand gestures when compared with the external control and more speech errors when compared with the internal control.

So do all these signs add up to lying all the time?

We need to note a few caveats. For example, these signs of deception are "symptom clusters," and a single sign does not a liar make. However, we can also say that the greater the number of these signs, the greater the likelihood of mendacity. Certain vocal issues, like stuttering or hesitant speech, may indicate patterns that aren't linked to deception.

If and when you're thinking about factors within this material that apply to you, it's important to remember that in any single discussion, the presence of the 23 signs proves nothing, and their frequency must be compared with that of a truthful control period. If possible, it's preferable that the truthful control period occurs in the same environment as the deceptive period to eliminate such confounding factors as a stressful environment.

Furthermore, the communication type should be the same, because the means of communication alone may affect the frequency of these signs. For example, pauses may occur more frequently in question-and-answer-style speech (interrogatory) than in prepared speech. That means that interrogatory truthful periods should be compared with interrogatory deceptive periods. In our study, we had control speech both from the same environment and communication type (a prepared speech as the external control).

Looking at Results

Overall, our results may err on the conservative side. The truthful internal control period occurred at the start of the testimony, and it's likely that anticipatory anxiety caused a fairly high level of stress at the start. That means that the baseline level of stress during this control period may have been elevated. That would minimize the differences between the deceptive and honest periods, and the signs of deception may have been less marked than if we had chosen another portion of his testimony as the baseline control.

In terms of methodology, we weren't able to verify the veracity of the presumed-truthful periods. We had to assume that President Clinton was telling the truth during the fund-raising speech, as well as during the internal control in the deposition, that is, when he was giving answers to routine factual questions from which a lie would be easily detected, such as the name of his attorney. If, in fact, he was not being truthful during these periods, our results actually underestimated the changes associated with lying.

The question of stress

It's certainly true that stress alone may generate some of the 23 signs in certain areas: speech, for example. When we're under stress we tend to change our words mid-sentence, and we add many "uhs" and "ahs." The moral ambivalence associated with lying generates internal conflict and induces a stress reaction. Failure to differentiate between a pure stress response and deception is known as the "Othello error." If what we observed had been merely a stress response (and not lying), we would still find more of the signs during the testimony period than during the other low-stress speech. However, we would not see as many signs during the period later found to be deceptive as during the truthful period of the same high-stress testimony.

Another caveat

Objective signs are not reliable indicators when evaluating pathologic liars. Persons who do not hold a moral code against the transgression of lying (a moral "lacune") do not display the signs. That's why some people are able to lie with such a smooth delivery. In addition, those who can convince themselves that their lies are truthful do not display the signs. Similarly, psychotic patients who believe their delusions do not display these signs. Certain professionals, such as actors and politicians, have trained themselves to lie, and they can hide many of the associated signs and even display misleading feelings. Actors trained in the Stanislavski method, for example, can present a character in a particular way by evoking emotional memories.

Among those who perceive lying to be immoral, deliberate deception triggers internal or unconscious conflict, which is shown through symbolic actions. For example, if I cover my mouth or cross my legs or make Freudian slips, I would be symbolically preventing the lies. If I fidget with my eyeglasses, I may be showing an unconscious symbol of manipulating the person I'm lying to.

Untruthful responses are more hesitant than truthful ones, and this hesitancy may be manifested by stammering, stalling maneuvers, empty words, modifiers, and qualifiers. The need to think and

Lip Tightening: To prevent the lie from escaping.

consider one's words can cause delays, but lying requires greater cognitive effort than telling the truth.

The emotional center of the brain (the limbic lobe) and facial muscles in expression may be connected in a predetermined pattern that only a concentrated effort can override. What that means is that although a lying person can control his or her words, the face reveals the truth. For example, a sidelong smile may express the incongruity of speech and facial expression.

Similarly, lying influences the chemical messengers in the brain, and these influence body movements and reactions, such as frequent blinking and random movement of the hands and feet. The Pinocchio phenomenon can cause discomfort in that the nasal engorgement causes irritation and itching, and that's what leads to scratching the nose. Dry mouth can result from reduced saliva, which makes the throat become dry, and the person's voice grow hoarse. Even the tongue may protrude and become dry, and that leads to reaching for the glass of water.

You Don't Need to Bring in a Polygraph Machine

Unlike the polygraph or other technologies that require extensive equipment, the 23 signs I've described can be assessed with observation. Some might find this watching and evaluating a bit distracting, but, with practice, it will become second nature—and you will be able to identify lies all around you. Use the illustrations included here as a guide, a way to match what you see with what we understand about physical and verbal signs of deception.

However, this skill does take practice. You can liken this to being a psychiatrist in residency training. A psychiatrist learns during residency training to determine how sick a patient is and whether he requires hospitalization, such that it soon becomes second nature. Eventually, when a psychiatric patient appears in the emergency room, the resident is able to determine the need for admission within the first 30 seconds of meeting the patient. Similarly, over time, you can become a human lie detector.

First, practice—listen and categorize as your family, friends, and co-workers talk. It is hard to learn, process, and evaluate while thinking about the context of the conversation or how you are supposed to respond to the discussion, so you'll be listening more than talking. If you must think of a response, you can't concentrate on the signs of lying. So until you have mastered these techniques, use them only while acting as an observer in the conversation, or while sitting in an otherwise boring meeting, for instance. Soon, this evaluation will be second nature, like tying your shoes. When you were a child, you had to think out each step, but now you can talk about politics or ask what's for dinner or do math in your head while you're tying your shoes. With time, the same will be true for your lie-detecting ability. Once you have mastered this process, it will be time to evaluate the best liars, better than the CIA, KGB, terrorists, FBI, or even lawyers—your teenage children!

Chapter 5

Making a Federal Case out of It, or Why Does This Matter Anyway?

I'm taking another detour. Why? Because whenever we begin to get down to the nitty-gritty of teens and lying, I've become aware that parents have a tendency to retreat and minimize. You may be tempted to close this book and tell yourself you don't really need it—other parents could benefit, but not you. You have a handle on how things are going with your kids. Their lies are just about the little stuff—finishing homework or not doing their chores before calling a friend.

Since I began working on this book, I especially noticed the tendency to retreat and fall into self-deception. All the dismissive comments parents make became amplified. Things I might not have noticed suddenly came into focus and sounded significant, and in their way, alarming. Most comments fall into the category of self-reassurance. Surely, the lying their kids engage in can't be so bad. Okay, maybe Bobby cheated on a test or Barbara lied about smoking cigarettes at a party—and that was after she denied even being at the party. But, all that's normal, not serious. Right? No sense "making a federal case out of it."

Back in my youth, this expression about "making a federal case" always applied to our parents getting upset over something one of their kids did—no matter how slight or serious. Whatever it was, we considered it "no big deal." Our parents might have thought otherwise, but sometimes they, ultimately, let the problem slip by. That's what parents often do.

Parents minimize for a few reasons. Like the kids, we may say:

- "All kids do it, so these little lies can't be so bad."

- "At least she/he isn't lying about _____!"

- "I trust him/her about the big things, so I let the little things go."

- "If I press too hard, she/he will clam up and I won't get any information."

- "I try not to ask questions if I'm afraid to hear the answers to them."

- "She/he promised never to do it again, so I'm taking my child's word."

All those statements, and many others like them, are common and based on the need to tell ourselves the best version of the story. Unfortunately, our own egos are entwined with our kids', and when they do wrong, we have a tendency to believe we've done something wrong. Therefore, we tell ourselves lies to protect our own self-image.

The underlying lie we tell ourselves is that *whatever the kids are doing or lying about isn't really all that important because we've done a good job and they're basically good kids.* In essence, parents try to disassociate what their kids say or do from deception. This is where parents are the biggest danger to their kids. It's where our failures threaten their futures.

In order to see the big picture, the idea of separating the trivial from the important, we need to look beyond the notion of lying to the greater issue of negativity and defiance. Too often, parents ignore this behavior, too, in order to avoid confrontations that sometimes seem pointless. They may look at their child as if he or she has become alien and unreachable. But pay attention to this negative communication, regardless of its content.

The Look of Deception? Maybe Not

In the previous chapter, I talked about verbal and physical signs of lying. But since teens aren't adults, they have some negative (usually) body language of their own that may—or may not—point to deception. For example, teens tend to become impatient with adults, and they might show that as boredom; defiance may come off as sarcasm and minimizing. So, while you're studying body language to detect deception, I suggest paying attention to what your teens may be communicating on other levels and about other issues.

Here are some clues, which *may or may not point to lying,* but which may reflect resistance, at the least. You know something is going awry with a conversation when you see some of these expressions and gestures:

Eye rolling: Kids are big on this because it's something they believe they can get away with. It falls short of "smarting off." It's linked with a sarcastic reaction, and is meant to diminish what a parent is saying as ridiculous or even outlandish!

It's a silent way of saying, *Oh, please, do you really think that I'd go to a party where _____ is going on?*

The smirk or twisted smile: Again, these body language cues may be part of deflecting what you're saying. It's a defiant expression and indicates that the child is brushing off your words as too ridiculous to take seriously. In adults it may look like simple sarcasm, but in a

teenager it says, *You think you know everything, Dad, but I'm smarter than you think.*

Nervous tapping and such: Kids aren't always comfortable in their own skin. They may want to argue, but may not be able to find the right words, or they're afraid of saying too much. So your child may tap

one foot, maybe while chewing the lower lip. Again, he or she may not be engaged in a lying situation, but he or she clearly doesn't want to talk. You child is communicating a message that goes something like this: *You can make me sit here and listen, but I don't want to be here and I'm not going to talk to you.*

This nervous tapping and chewing can also indicate a fear of being caught at something. Perhaps he or she has denied doing something forbidden or he or she is afraid of being found out doing something wrong.

Folded arms, shrugging, hands on hips: Typically, in both adults and kids, these physical gestures indicate an unwilling-ness to give much in terms of points. In kids, they may indicate feigned indifference: *I really don't care what you think.* Hands planted on the hips can  also be an indication of anger while saying words that try to com-municate an attitude of indifference.

The tight mouth: We may see this along with things like folded arms or tapping feet. Like the other expressions, it indi-cates holding back or defiantly refusing to find common ground with you.

Lightening Up the Conversation

We sometimes forget that raising children is supposed to include some fun and light-hearted moments. It sometimes seems that as we march through the childhood years, we have less fun as the kids get older. Part of our role as parents is passing on family stories and lore, and enjoying our kids as they learn new things and tell us the riddles and jokes they learn. There's something enormously gratifying and enjoyable about watching our children's wonder at the world as they ask their questions and take in knowledge. It's fun to see our much-loved babies take their first steps or listen to them read aloud to us from their first books.

It's true that our job may get tougher as the kids get older, but sometimes we can combat the surly and sullen behavior reflected in the conversations above with "tricks" of verbal and nonverbal communication. We can attempt to recapture the feelings, if not the content, of earlier shared good times. Try these strategies to lighten the mood in your household when the adolescent doldrums have set in:

Matching and mirroring: While it doesn't always work, the occasional spontaneous and exaggerated matching behavior may work to change the "air in the room" If your teen smirks, smirk back—and in a big way. Roll your eyes to make sure your teen knows that you know what she's up to. Hey, try it, and you may even draw a begrudging laugh. You won't solve the problem, but you will allow some old rapport to be reestablished.

Matching and mirroring techniques work "for real," too. If your child is leaning against the kitchen counter with her arms crossed over her chest, then lean against the stove and cross your arms, too. This isn't meant to manipulate, but rather, send a message of compatibility. Sales professionals and others, including doctors and lawyers, may unconsciously or consciously use this subtle mirroring technique.

Once rapport is established, you'll notice that these mirroring techniques begin automatically. In friendly conversations, people's hands and arms move in synchrony and sometimes postures seem to form in a way that mirrors the other's posture.

Allowing and removing: Sometimes you can change the tone by ignoring the rolling eyes and the tapping feet. Just allow it to be, and don't comment on it. Say your piece and leave. By removing yourself from the situation, you allow your teenagers to save face. You also avoid watching the defiant act of her walking out on you. This kind of action reduces immediate anger, and you can reopen the conversation later.

What Is Our Real Job?

In the previous chapters I described what people in the fields of psychiatry and psychology know about lying, and I also offered information about the potential to detect lying behavior by watching for verbal signs and body language. By now I imagine you're thinking that preventing and uncovering deceptive behavior in teens sounds like a really daunting task. When I began linking what I know about lying to my own role as a parent, it left me exhausted, too. Yet, I'm aware that it's so important to determine if and when my kids are engaging in deceptive behavior, no matter how small or insignificant it might appear. But why? For example, why would a child's lie about whether she finished her homework or he folded his laundry be important enough to cause concern?

As parents, we have an obligation to think beyond today, which is a sign of our maturity as adults. Considering consequences beyond the moment is an acquired ability. Very small children don't have it, and many teens have yet to have a fully developed handle on the concept of the future. This is precisely why it's important to keep children honest about what they're doing. We must provide the judgment that our kids lack.

Another one of our jobs as parents is to build character in our children. We hope we don't have to do this alone, but that extended family, schools, and religious communities are on hand to help. Still, this is primarily our responsibility. So it's both our burden and our privilege to pass on our moral code to the next generation, and that's far more critical than grooming or shaping our kids to be popular or to win academic awards or break sports records. Over the long term, our true job is to raise individuals of sound character, young people who become contributing citizens, not just consumers.

Sometimes, especially in the midst of all the work involved with raising children, it can seem as if the days become consumed with school, sports, and social activities. Today's children are probably the most scheduled of any in recent history—some say over-scheduled. In fact, one reason many parents keep children so busy is to steer them away from the myriad temptations lurking around every corner. But that doesn't mean that "busy-ness" builds a child's sense of ethical behavior.

We can't count on packed schedules. We need to become lie detectors, too. Why? Because the risks are great and the consequences too devastating to ignore.

Remembering What Your Children Face

I touched on it at the beginning of this book, but it bears repeating that drug and alcohol addiction in the U.S. affects more and more young people every day. Our country's so-called "War on Drugs" and the various anti-drug campaigns that have gone on for many years may have a positive influence on some young people. That's all for the good, but it's not typical, and we haven't healed anything.

While the numbers vary, based on data the government and private organizations collect, it's clear that we've made marginal and fragile progress in combating alcohol and drug abuse and subsequent addiction among young people. According to the American Academy of Pediatrics and the Centers for Disease Control and Prevention (CDC), in 2007 almost two-thirds of high school seniors admitted using alcohol in the previous 30 days, and almost one-third said they'd had a drink in the past week. While the numbers are slightly less for drugs, almost one-third admitted to using marijuana in the past month. (I've listed web sites that offer information about these issues in the back of this book.) Sadly, the drug and alcohol issue not only remains with us, but it exists in virtually every community, from the most impoverished to the most affluent.

Frankly, in most poor communities, these problems are neither well-hidden nor denied. Parents openly talk about the threat to their children posed by drug and alcohol abuse on the street corner, the schoolyard, and down every alley. Parents in these communities may be well aware of other addictive or destructive substances and behaviors. In wealthier towns and neighborhoods, addiction and its attending problems may not be as visible, and, sadly, that allows too many parents to assume that the problem affects other families. It's easy to exclude ourselves from problems that we don't see directly. As a psychiatrist-neurologist, I know that no racial, ethnic, religious, or economic group can consider itself immune from mental illness, for example, and parents must understand that the same vulnerability applies to both chemical and behavioral addictions. I see the results of ignorance and denial every day in my medical practice.

Facing the Dangers

I mention the drug and alcohol issue first, because by the time your children are pre-teens they have learned a thing or two about both alcohol and drugs. Parents *must* be aware that their children may be offered alcohol or be around young people drinking. Nowadays, parents may be so concerned and even preoccupied with teaching their five-year-olds about the dangers of tobacco that they forget about the marijuana that they'll be exposed to before they're even teens. They may not think about the beer their kids' friends sneak out of their houses.

Whether your kids participate in drinking or drug use at a house down the street or in secret in your home, *their first instinct is to lie about it* if you ask them. I can see the innocent, eye-rolling denial now. Can't you? This is a sign of danger for you, because it may be where you may believe that you failed to prevent your child's misbehavior and subsequent lie. But not confronting your child is the bigger problem.

We can look at a couple of reasons that you must be willing to detect lies about any drug and alcohol exposure and use among pre-teens and teens. First, among kids, there is no such thing as casual drug and alcohol use. Alcohol poisoning and drug overdose—or accidents related to these things—kill young people every day. In addition, a downward cycle inevitably follows early use of alcohol and drugs. Risk of addiction is ever-present and real, and no ethnic or racial group is immune. (Later, I'll discuss the physiological reasons why early use of addictive substances is devastating to a child's development.) Second, we could devote our lives to eliminating importation and distribution of marijuana or heroin or cocaine, and still, we would not be successful in protecting our children from these drugs or from the oldest legal drug we know of, namely, alcohol. Yes, our society would be more peaceful and productive if we could break up the complex network involved in saturating our communities with illegal drugs, but we can't do this alone, and we most certainly can't do it quickly enough to make a difference for our children. Meanwhile, we must control what is within our circle of influence, our children.

I've learned that many parents lack some basic awareness of the kinds of substances that their kids can *easily* come across and experiment with. This idea of experimentation lulls parents into believing that this is somehow natural and harmless behavior, like experimenting in chemistry class. We should eliminate the word from our vocabulary. Besides, it has almost laughable class connotations: disadvantaged kids *use* drugs, but privileged kids *experiment* with them.

This topic of drugs and alcohol represents fertile ground in which to grow lies. These substances are so dangerous to young children and teens that you must educate yourself about them and then be prepared to be vigilant in your efforts to keep your kids away from them. And be prepared to detect lies concerning them!

Our Love-Hate Relationship with Alcohol

Every culture we know of, ancient and modern, distills some form of alcohol, which in moderation produces in many people a sense of relaxation or an enjoyable high. Wine is the drink of choice in the Bible (along with some cautionary talk about excess), so we know that ancient Middle-Eastern cultures included alcohol in their religious rituals, and we still see this across the globe among Jews and Christians alike.

Recently, a news magazine ran an article raising the idea that teaching young people to drink responsibly is one answer to the problem of heavily drinking teens. If, for example, parents drink wine with their meals, then the idea would be to let a teenager have wine with dinner, too, thereby demystifying alcohol. I'm wary of this idea for a couple of reasons, specifically because this would include the notion of drinking every day, which is not something we want to encourage in our kids. On the other hand, I do understand that certain cultures do include a drink or two of alcohol as part of daily life. As parents, we may respect other cultures and the way they teach drinking behavior to their kids, but in this country we're painfully aware of the out-of-control drinking so common among American youth. A middle ground may be to allow an older teen a small glass of wine with holiday meals. It could be considered a rite of passage within the family. (Under no circumstances should parents allow anyone else's children to drink in their own home.)

Looking at alcohol from a scientific and medical viewpoint, we know that alcohol is a mild depressant, which is why the first drink often relaxes and the third or fourth may cause sleepiness. Sometimes, especially among teens, a drink will turn on the energy spigot, at least for a while. It's also dangerous when used with other chemicals, such as tranquilizers or amphetamines.

Reality: Alcohol poisoning

Accidental death by excess alcohol consumption is a real concern, but parents too easily treat it as something that "can't happen to us." But alcohol can depress the brain to the point that the person slips into a coma and dies. Breathing can become depressed as well, also resulting in death. We used to associate drinking games with college kids, mostly fraternity boys. That's inaccurate, however. Today, girls are almost as likely to participate in this kind of public drunken behavior as boys. In addition, high school kids and even middle school kids may get their hands on alcohol and end up binging on alcohol as part of some lame game. If they drink alcohol "coolers," such as vodka mixed with fruit juice or soft drinks, they may not know how much they've consumed until it's too late and the alcohol in their blood reaches such a level that it's a poison.

Of course, as a parent you'd certainly want to discourage this behavior in your college-age kids, too, but you have less control over your kids by the time they reach that age. You can and must prevent your young children and teens from any exposure to alcohol, just as you must face the reality that driving under the influence occurs all too frequently among teens. Or let's put it this way: lying about being in a car with an impaired driver is serious, and detecting that lie may help you uncover other risky behavior going on—and you may save young lives in the process.

Marijuana (Tetrahydrocannabinol)

Misinformed or very naïve and gullible parents may buy into the street talk that pot, reefer, or weed is relatively harmless and kind of cool—and they'll tell you that this kind of drug use is common among adults, too. Oh, sure, the kids may admit that driving under the influence of marijuana is bad, but otherwise using it is "no big thing." Besides, to these kids (or adults), cooking up a batch of pot brownies is harmless. (Most marijuana is not typically ingested in food, however.)

Adults are most likely to use (and perhaps abuse) some prescription drugs and alcohol, but among the range of illegal substances, marijuana is probably the one most likely found in the so-called average home. It may surprise some of us, but some parents continue to use marijuana after they have children, despite being fully aware that it's illegal.

Kids and adults use marijuana for many reasons. It's relatively inexpensive and available virtually anywhere in the country. It's also said to be non-addictive and have fewer adverse affects than many drugs, such as alcohol. Frankly, some people who become troublesome and belligerent when they drink alcohol are mellow when they smoke pot. This is one important attraction of the drug.

Some claim that marijuana is not addictive and therefore not dangerous; others counter that position with data showing that it is addictive and, at least among young people, seldom used by itself. It has long been considered a "gateway drug," meaning that it leads to other substance abuse. (This isn't true 100% of the time, but that's irrelevant for this discussion. Kids may use this argument, but don't buy into it.) Because it's an anxiety-relieving drug, users of it often gradually need greater quantities in order to reach the same relaxed state. Unfortunately, for some individuals, pot smoking becomes a daily ritual, like popping a tranquilizer.

Those of us who grew up in the 1960s and '70s may have heard that marijuana is an "ambition killer," and that label countered its benign impression. The fact is, many of us observed individuals who seemed to gradually lose interest in their goals—perhaps sleeping too much or skipping classes in college. They would make plans, but rarely followed through with them. They were going to get themselves moving—tomorrow.

Watch for these behavioral signs in your children, even if you believe it's highly unlikely that they're using drugs. They may be depressed or overtired or troubled in some other way, so you can't jump to conclusions. But especially among middle-teens and those approaching college age, if they seem to have lost drive and ambition, then they may be secretly using marijuana.

I also recommend watching for (and listening for) these signs in their friends. Kids tend to do things in groups, and if some of your teens' friends are having problems or exhibit some evidence of drug use, then it's time to probe around and find out what's going on. You may notice that your teen isn't interested in certain friends anymore. That could mean he is moving away from other kids who are using marijuana, or he is using and is moving away from the kids who aren't.

The Under-Reported Inhalants

For some reason, many parents forget this type of substance abuse. For some, the practice of "sniffing" may seem outdated or, again, something "my kids" don't know anything about, and, therefore, it isn't a threat. However, a key characteristic of inhalants is their availability. Glue and spray paint are sold everywhere, although some restrictions have been applied to spray paint and the glue used in assembling model airplanes and cars. The point is, kids inhale the fumes of a variety of substances to experience a high, and that in itself is dangerous. Young people can become brain-damaged through this practice—and that's what parents often discount.

And We Can't Forget Steroids

Steroids can be a confusing topic because certain hormones, such as estrogen and testosterone, are naturally occurring steroids in the body. Cortisol, produced in the adrenal glands, is also a steroid. The steroids that fall into the category of "abused substances" are anabolic steroids, which are produced in a lab. These are dangerous because they add manufactured hormones to those naturally produced. Primarily we're talking about adding artificially produced testosterone, which is like giving males an extra dose of the male hormone.

We know because of many scandals in high school, college, and professional sports that steroid use is common and extremely dangerous. The only reason a young athlete would take steroids involves a desire to increase athletic strength and increase muscle mass in a misguided effort to look like a body builder. Your child's school may have programs to both educate and detect anabolic steroid use. Your child's coach should be able to watch for increased acne or hair loss or personality changes—the infamous "roid rage" we know exists. Over the long term, anabolic steroid use can lead to sterility and severe liver damage. There's no such thing as "harmless" steroid experimentation.

Other Drugs to Consider

U.S. streets are awash with drugs that go in and out of the public eye. Unfortunately, they go in and out of fashion, too. For years, *cocaine* (a stimulant) was the drug of choice for kids when marijuana began to be viewed as too tame. In the 1980s, it made headlines as the drug of choice for risk-takers and "high-rollers" such as day traders and others working in the frantic atmosphere of the financial markets or in other glamorous occupations, like the entertainment industry. The inexpensive form of cocaine, known as "crack," showed up on city streets—and there it has stayed. It wreaks havoc on kids and on families and on whole communities. To use it is to become involved in an underground network of illegal activities, and that's what damages communities where the sellers and buyers must find ways to hook up.

Cocaine in its various forms is highly addictive, which is why we hear horror stories about miserable lives that revolve around the quest for more of the drug. Even high rollers can end up criminals or prostitutes. Young people may become one of the armies of runaways and "street kids" because of the ravages of addiction to this drug.

Among kids, signs that they're using this drug could include the loss of interest in school or sports or even a social life. Cocaine users tend to lose weight, too, because they don't experience normal hunger and a drive to eat. Cocaine use can also result in heart damage and overall deteriorating health. Kids using this drug will most certainly lie about it—and eventually, they'll lie about everything else.

Among the other drugs that kids and adults abuse, amphetamines (and similar drugs) probably top the list. These are stimulants and are sometimes used legitimately to stay awake and alert, but they also have a checkered history as an aid in weight loss.

These days, we hear a great deal about the devastating effects of methamphetamine, commonly called "meth" or "crystal meth." This addictive drug is inhaled and produces a very quick high. TV reports regularly focus on meth labs, often within homes and garages in small communities and rural areas. It's an easy drug for amateurs to produce in these makeshift labs, but the drug also destroys families and has a demoralizing effect on communities.

Invariably, when meth labs are around, the crime rate goes up. One kind of illegal and secretive activity usually increases other illegal actions. It is well known among addiction specialists (and those who have ever struggled to overcome addiction, especially to an illegal substance) that those who use illegal drugs tend to gravitate to each other, creating an atmosphere of deception and, ultimately, criminal activity. Methamphetamine users and those addicted to other drugs gradually blur the boundaries between right and wrong, and often exhibit a kind of defiant bravado. Inevitably, drugs that harm the body and brain eventually reduce the capacity for good judgment. It's not likely that a person taking meth will show good judgment on the job for very long, for example, and, like many alcoholics, they eventually have trouble even showing up for work. The resulting unemployment and poverty almost always leads to greater crime rates. I believe that meth use among kids can sneak up on parents everywhere, but especially in small towns that seem so far away from the image of back-alley drug use associated with cities.

You may have heard that pseudophedrine, an ingredient in over-the-counter cold medicines (such as Sudafed®), is also an ingredient used in manufacturing crystal meth. Therefore, many states now monitor and control the sale of these cold medications. The problem with banning or monitoring a cold medication, however, is that lives are already destroyed before the society can catch up with the damage. In other words, you don't want to be a parent who appears on a TV show to warn other parents about a problem that harmed your child and your family.

The Ugliness of "Heroin Chic"

If you've heard the expression "heroin chic," then you are aware of another street drug that's highly addictive and ruins lives. A few decades ago, only musicians or a certain so-called "underclass" of individuals ended up as heroin addicts. Now we see famous models and actors and other stars go off to rehab because heroin use has escalated and addiction results. The term "heroin chic" also refers to a look commonly seen in young models that are so thin they appear wasted and even ill. In some cases, these young models are staying so thin because they use heroin to depress appetite. Heroin promotes the gaunt, bony look they crave. Fortunately, the trend of super-thin models may be easing, and sanity may return.

Heroin is a highly addictive illegal drug and may not be readily available to young people in every corner of the country. However, I recommend finding out if the drug is making its way into your community. Heroin is not a common "gateway" drug, but is one that people who have used other drugs may gravitate to over time. If you learn that your child has used heroin, then you will need to investigate to see what other drugs he or she has been using.

Heroin is in a class of drugs known as opiates, and some other opiates may have legitimate medical uses, primarily to relieve pain or coughing. Examples include morphine, demerol, codeine, and hydrocodone. Methadone is also an opiate we associate with helping heroin addicts wean themselves off the drug.

The Designer Drugs

Ecstasy is a manufactured drug that seems to rise and fall in popularity. Drugs like this spread into communities if they can be distributed cheaply and without a high risk of detection. You often find ecstasy at concerts and large gatherings of kids. While not addicting, it alters mental function, like the infamous hallucinogenic LSD (lysergic acid diethylamide), or "acid."

Another hallucinogen, PCP (phencyclidine), commonly known as "angel dust," became popular among young people in the 1970s. It's very dangerous because it's a hallucinogen, has an anesthetic effect, and also acts as a stimulant. Talk about a drug that affects judgment!

Obviously, many of these drugs have been around for a long time, and today's parents may have either known about them or used them, too, and most have since regretted it. Even if they believe they came out of that period unharmed, they may be doubly protective of their children and try even harder to prevent their drug use.

Don't Forget the Medicine Cabinet

Some drug abuse among young people today occurs because they get their hands on prescription drugs, either from their parents' medicine cabinet or via the Internet. Among the most commonly used are the tranquilizers and sleeping medications such as Xanax®, Librium®, Ativan®, Transene®, Valium®, Dalmane™, and Halcion™. Newer sleeping medications include the much-advertised Ambien® and Sonata®. These drugs reduce anxiety and may also produce a euphoric reaction, and when a doctor orders a sedative, it's usually this type of drug. It's not unusual to become addicted to these drugs. In fact, prescription drug addiction is on the rise. These drugs have a variety of characteristics, and certain groups of individuals, such as recovering alcoholics, must avoid them.

You may have heard that cough medicine and other cold medications are in the news because kids have learned to abuse them. Dextromethorphan is an ingredient in some over-the-counter (OTC) preparations, such as Robitussin® DM and NyQuil®. Kids take these OTC products in large quantities to get a euphoric high and as a hallucinogen. This misuse is dangerous because these products are safe only when used properly, and some teens deliberately set out to misuse them. This is another of the "group think" activities. Kids generally don't go off to find NyQuil to use alone.

What you need to be aware of is that some young people have taken up the practice of raiding the medicine cabinet, or the bolder among them order these drugs from the Internet using fraudulent means. Kids tend to be quite collegial about this kind of activity and share the goods when they get them. That's why you must be vigilant, even if you don't have prescription or even many OTC drugs in your home.

The List Wouldn't Be Complete Without Nicotine

We find nicotine, a highly addicting substance, in tobacco. At one time, nicotine was considered safe when used in tobacco products such as cigarettes and cigars. No more. We know, your kids know, everyone in the country, if not the world, knows that nicotine is addictive and the products it's found in have the potential to destroy health and lead to premature death.

In recent years, cigarette smokers and those who chew tobacco (and to a lesser extent pipe and cigar smokers) have begun to use the word "addict" to describe themselves. Nicotine addiction is a medical issue, and there are treatments for it. Still, for some kids, cigarette smoking holds a strong appeal, and tobacco has mild mental effects that smokers say relieve anxiety and help them concentrate. In actuality, it has very little effect other than its addicting qualities.

Fortunately, in a non-smoking family, the kids have trouble hiding cigarette smoking. We can smell it on them and in their clothes. While kids are not smoking at such alarming rates as they did even a decade ago, you can bet they'll lie about it if they're playing around with tobacco.

What You Must Know about Your Child's Brain

A variety of addicting drugs and hallucinogens, along with alcohol, pose a big threat to our kids. For generations, kids and parents have been engaged in a dance of lies and deception about these substances, but because of their great availability today, detecting any lying behavior around them is critical. For example:

"Was there alcohol at the dance?"

"Huh? No, there was not!" (Such indignation at the question! Arms immediately cross in front of body.)

"None?"

"Uh, well, Joe thought about it." (A quick aversion of eyes, a glance down at the floor.)

"Thought about it? But he didn't bring any?"

"Oh, well, maybe."

This kind of weak conversation goes on and on, and sometimes parents find out that "someone" did indeed bring alcohol to a dance. These awkward exchanges have a common thread: the kids lie outright, or, when pressed, they minimize or tell only part of the story, and they almost always claim that they weren't involved—they didn't know a thing!

Most parents tend to back off at some point. They believe (mistakenly) that if they keep pressing, they'll just drive their son or daughter into a corner and no information will be forthcoming. Sometimes they back off because they don't really want to know the answer, and they may vow to themselves that they'll be much more careful the next time a dance rolls around. But these awkward answers coupled with his or her "shuffling around" body language demand further attention.

At some point, your child is going to be given the chance to take his or her first drink or first drug. I don't care if your child is five or ten years old today, this is an eventuality to prepare for now. This is where too many of us fail our kids.

Not only are these conversation about chemical substances often riddled with lies, which is serious enough, but we have hard scientific evidence that early use of addicting substances can have tragic consequences. So being able to detect lies takes on special importance, because *your child's brain depends on it.*

The Young, Developing Brain

Because of improved technology, we have begun to unravel the mysteries of the brain, including children's brain development. Briefly, the brain is the control center of the CNS—central nervous system—which functions as a kind of "operating system" for the body. We are able to breathe, dance, drive, learn languages, and do higher math because of the CNS. We can walk and chew gum at the same time we're digesting dinner, because the CNS doesn't stop working for even one millisecond until we die. We have numerous types of differentiated cells in the body, including specialized brain and nervous system cells called neurons. Some neurons are involved in memory and some in motor skills and others in detecting odors or sounds or sights.

The communication system among neurons is one of the most complex of all bodily functions, but, simply put, neurons have structural components that send or receive information; they send information through axons and receive it through dendrites. This is part of the electrical activity of the brain, which is sometimes illustrated with a series of lights showing how cells fire and transmit information. Information is transmitted from neuron to neuron from the axon of one cell to the dendrite of another across a space we call the synapse. The synapses are like microscopic traffic cops that are always on duty to direct information to the correct axon with its chemical receptors at the ready. Neurotransmitters are the brain chemicals involved in sending information.

You've no doubt heard about neurotransmitters because we see an ever-growing number of medications for numerous diseases, from depression to Parkinson's disease to Alzheimer's disease, that work to promote or inhibit the body's production of certain neurotransmitters. Some of these neurotransmitters, like serotonin or dopamine, have become household words, so to speak, and even your teens may have a working understanding that many disorders are treated by correcting chemical imbalances.

We can treat depression, for example, with effective medications that manipulate neurotransmitters. However, when it comes to preventing a disease like depression or obsessive-compulsive disorder or Alzheimer's, we don't have great knowledge or tools. With chemical addiction, though, we find ourselves in the opposite situation. We don't have good chemical agents to treat it or reverse the damage it does, but we *do know how to prevent it*.

Wait, Just Wait!

Obviously, never using a substance prevents addiction. If you don't smoke, you won't get hooked on nicotine. But beyond that, today we understand that brain maturation is also involved in preventing addiction. Or put another way, the developing brain is vulnerable, and exposing it to addicting substances increases its chances to become addicted. This is why we rarely hear about a college senior, who has never used tobacco, suddenly deciding that smoking cigarettes would be an excellent idea. Statistics clearly show that if you don't try a cigarette until you're an adult, you probably won't become addicted to nicotine. Cigarette companies know this, which is why they created cartoon-like advertising gimmicks to appeal to teens. Remember the friendly and cute image of Joe Camel?

A 12-year-old who has a first exposure to nicotine often has an entirely different reaction—the immature brain decides that smoking is a really cool thing to do. (The exception to this rule occurs among soldiers, whose need for a socially acceptable and immediate way of relieving stress may override judgment. Many soldiers in WWII and Vietnam began smoking during their service, when the dangers were less established. But even our younger military recruits may be vulnerable to taking up cigarette smoking for the same reasons as their grandfathers, even though the dangers are well documented.)

The link between the age of first-use of a chemical and addiction is truly revolutionary knowledge. Our information remains incomplete, but, viewed as a whole, scientific evidence shows us that early first use resulting in inebriation or a high (any state of altered consciousness) *permanently* changes the brain and represents a major risk for addiction, with all its attending problems. (See the list of recommended books and articles for more information about that research.) And remember, we don't have a cure for chemical addiction. The best we can do is help patients understand their addiction and recommend abstinence programs, primarily 12-step recovery fellowships.

No matter what treatment is sought, two of the areas of the brain, the nucleus accumbens and the frontal cortex, are altered forever. These areas are critical to well-being, because they direct things like motivation and decision making. No wonder marijuana seems like an ambition killer or those using alcohol over time lose everything. The young brain needs time to develop the capacity for higher functions, like judgment, the ability to evaluate situations, plan for the future, and solve problems.

When we hear about young adults who can't manage to put their lives together, no matter how hard the parents try to nudge them out of the nest, we may wonder what their problem is. Why can't they just do what normal, young adults do and take charge of themselves? We can't say for certain that the reason involves early first use of psychotropic substances, but it's certainly a good possibility, especially today, when so many kids have access to mind-altering substances.

Once addicted to alcohol or drugs (or certain behaviors, such as gambling), addicts' lives and the lives of everyone around them are never the same. That's why detecting lies or half-truths or other forms of deceptive behavior in your teens is essential. It's a major tool to *prevent* chemical addiction, one of the most serious medical and psychological problems our society faces.

Bring on the Awkward Conversations

When I used the sample conversation above, it was to illustrate the kind of dead-end we can reach with kids. Sometimes it seems that the conversations are circular, and we don't walk away either reassured or with much information in hand. Too many of us throw up our hands and figure that as long as Johnny and Jane are home safe and sound, then maybe it doesn't matter too much if we got the whole story. This is the critical failure. In actuality, the details of this party may be critical to what happens to your child next week, next month, or next year.

What's the Payoff?

Like adults, children are pleasure-seekers. We're designed that way, and the survival of our species depends on it. The force of life continues and evolves because we seek pleasure in sex and food and conversation. Babies seek the pleasure of nursing and being held. Five-year-olds (and 50-year-olds) are big fans of ice cream. We experience the pleasure because neurotransmitters send pleasure signals, and even thinking about the pleasure of meeting up with a lover may trigger an anticipatory pleasure response.

In scientific terms, the pleasure response occurs in the ventral tegmental area (VTA), a part of the brain located deep in its center. If we were to damage the VTA, we would no longer experience pleasure, a bleak situation indeed. We'd lose interest in chocolate or spending money, and we wouldn't look forward to a relaxing drink. Addiction would be unknown, because the euphoria—the high—or altered state of consciousness experienced with drugs and alcohol (and the rush felt by those addicted to certain behaviors) would not occur. We also know from animal studies that if we stimulate the VTA of rats, for example, with addicting substances, the rats will crave more and more of the chemicals. Like humans, these lab rats lose interest in everything except the addicting substance—the drug.

Creating this kind of addiction involves stimulating the VTA, and the neurotransmitter dopamine, which is associated with it. Dopamine is involved in managing or alleviating anxiety and producing euphoria, and its actions in the pleasure center of the brain help create addiction. Substances vary in the rapidity with which this occurs. Alcohol may take a period of many years, whereas crack or meth may result in an intense compulsion in a very short time; some say addiction can occur after the first use.

You may be familiar with stages of addiction, but if you're not, I urge you to educate yourself about the nature of addictive disease. (See the resource list.) What you need to know is that seemingly harmless experimentation may serve to prime the brain, actually setting it up for addiction.

How Did This Happen?

The reason any of this is important is that the science points to the idea that addictions are created during childhood and teen years. We also believe that, while some genetic predisposition exists, no one is immune. So no matter how squeaky clean your family seems to be when it comes to obvious chemical addictions, your children are vulnerable.

You may recall a concept known as *imprinting*, brought to us by biologist Konrad Lorenz. He showed that hours after birth, geese (and other birds) identified a moving stimulus as "mother." In other words, if a gosling saw a human face, then that face became "mother." Surviving photos show geese following behind Lorenz because these geese were imprinted with the concept of him as their mother. Although the human brain is more complex, it, too, is influenced by early stimuli, thus being imprinted with a concept. The young brain is open to receive and learns rapidly, always being imprinted with new ideas and information. This is both good and bad news. For example, viewing both loving and violent behavior and gestures are absorbed by the child and influence his or her personality. Physical and sexual abuse imprint and influence future thoughts and beliefs.

Likewise, chemicals, from airplane glue to alcohol to crack cocaine, imprint a developing brain. Time and time again, I've seen situations in which the kids who began drinking in their early high school years (or sooner) tend to get into trouble and develop addictions. The kids who are not exposed to these substances until their college years, or even late high school, tend to pass through the "wild oats" stage without engaging in binge drinking, for example, and they are less likely to develop addictions.

This is why it's our job as parents to be watchdogs and lie detectors. There is no such thing as safe, early use of certain drugs that produce a powerful and fast high, and, the younger a child's brain is exposed to one of these addicting chemicals, the more devastating it can be. Beyond that, the age of first high or euphoria is critical, too.

To illustrate, consider that Christian or Jewish children (generally age 12 or 13 and up) may take small sips of alcohol in religious rituals; in certain cultures, young people may drink some wine with their dinner. This small amount of alcohol is not intended to, nor does it, produce inebriation and therefore doesn't alter the brain. On the other hand, if someone gives those same children a joint or spikes their drink with many ounces of alcohol and their thought processes and behavior are altered, then we say they've experienced a high or are inebriated. This chemical experience can alter forever the young, developing brain.

More evidence

It seems that medicine is catching up to neurological science, and doctors and their patients will benefit if we're smart enough to pay attention. *The Archives of Pediatric and Adolescent Medicine* (July 2006) has reported that, based on an extensive study, those who begin *drinking alcohol before age 14 have a 50% chance of becoming an alcoholic*. This is as true in wealthy communities as it is in poor ones.

What a Combination

Adolescence is a time of contradictions. Teenagers are not small kids and can often be entrusted with important jobs and advanced learning tasks. We allow many teenagers to babysit, and they are perfectly capable of interpreting historical facts and forming opinions and learning calculus. We can have a conversation with a 16-year-old in which many seemingly adult concepts are analyzed. This often fools us into thinking that the adolescent brain is more or less the same as an adult brain. Unfortunately, they seem more adult than they actually are.

The immature brain is responsible for many of the traits we associate with adolescence. Why would your level-headed child speed on a back road, leave a party with a stranger or openly defy your rules? The immature brain in the grown-up body can lead him or her into such trouble. While it's true that many full-grown adults engage in risky behavior, it may occur as a result of an "out of character" impulse or, in some cases, because the person's brain is not fully developed. Teenagers who use drugs and alcohol at an early age may inhibit or permanently alter brain development. It's possible that many of today's reckless adults were reckless teens, and so their brains literally have not fully matured.

Teens feel immortal, which is a characteristic of their developmental age and is why they take risks in their cars. They are impulsive, which puts a negative and even dangerous spin on their natural and healthy adventurousness—and that's why they do stupid things like leave parties with strangers. They crave independence, so they rebel against your rules even when they don't gain much from it. They do it because they think they can. Besides, adult life looks really great compared to the corrals they feel trapped in.

We take our eyes off our teens at not only their peril, but ours as well. A lie about the bottle of vodka Joe brought to the party can lead to vandalism, accidents, or worse. Sometimes it can lead to arrests and lawsuits. And all because we let an adult-looking adolescent with a still-developing brain and immature thought processes get away with a lie. We didn't probe to find out what our children and their friends were really up to.

In some cases, we get into trouble because we're too trusting. Now, it's probably true that you had an approach-avoidance situation when you picked up this book. You didn't want to have to entertain the notion that your child is likely to lie to you—and perhaps already is lying to you on a regular basis. But this dilemma isn't about judging your child as much as it is about recognizing that your child still has a ways to go before reaching full maturation.

Back to nicotine

For some kids, drinking and using marijuana are far more accept-able than developing that "filthy" smoking habit. We've gone a bit topsy-turvy here, because moralizing over cigarette smoking may come through louder than the cautions about underage drinking. Although not as immediately dangerous as drinking, the long-term effects are serious, as you know. We know that nicotine is very addictive—one of the most highly addictive drugs in existence. It may also act to prime the pump, that is, set up a young brain for addiction. For this reason alone, it's of critical importance that you make sure your child does not smoke cigarettes or cigars—or use chewing tobacco, as some athletes do.

Smoking rates among kids rise and fall, but without a doubt, teens who smoke regularly become addicted. They also lie about smoking—in fact, they may be more fearful that you'll catch them using tobacco than sneaking some beer with their friends.

This is not an either-or situation. All these substances carry great immediate and long-term risks. Addiction to anything can be devastating.

If nothing else in this book convinces you that you must learn to discern if your teenager is lying, I hope this discussion of addiction and the developing brain has done it. So, yes, "make a federal case" out of anything that could point to lies and deceptive behavior. It's a very big deal!

Chapter 6

The Type of Lie May Confuse Us

As we've seen, your teens may lie about certain important, very big things. Anything involving drugs, alcohol, sex, and a few other areas is significant, and the behavior must be monitored. As a general rule, kids lie when they want to hide something or as a cover of some kind. They may lie if they perceive a greater value in it; for example getting a fake ID is an expedient lie and is worth it because a greater value is perceived. It's also justified by claiming that the stupid laws that establish a legal drinking age are unfair. Adults also lie out of self-interest, but also to enhance their perceived value. Among adults in our society, the most common lie involves age. According to the Internet dating service, eHarmony.com, substantially more men claimed to be 36 years old than statistically possible. But, *800% more* women claimed to be 29 years old than was statistically possible.

In addition to looking at the types of lies, we also need to recognize that, while all teenagers lie, some are better liars than others. Like adults, not all teenagers or younger children are equally facile at the art of deception. Their ability to lie is based on their intrinsic personalities, motivations, experiences, and the contents of the lies.

The Lying Personality

Another factor that may derail your parental lie detector is if your child has what we can call "a lying personality," meaning outgoing and gregarious, a social extrovert who enjoys manipulating others, perhaps by telling entertaining stories. Of course, this doesn't mean that all those with a special talent for social interactions tell lies, but these individuals have the tendency to make use of the small fib or tall tale.

As adults, those with these traits may gravitate to occupations such as sales, where a certain degree of fibbing, exaggerating, deception, or simply stretching the truth is not just accepted and tolerated, but is even expected. The law attracts this same personality type, too. I was inspired to investigate the proficiency of lying, because I was intrigued by the idea that those good at deception might enter the same professions.

Although it sounds odd, I decided to look specifically at one group of liars, lawyers, in a test of the capacity to lie, in this case, regarding olfactory ability. (Olfaction is the medical term for the sense of smell.) Specifically, we conducted this experiment with law students in Judge Steven Schiller's class at Loyola University Law School in Chicago, Illinois.

Although it may sound odd to test a person's ability to smell, especially in relation to the propensity to lie, part of a standard neurologic examination includes testing the patient's ability to smell. Doing so is strongly recommended because many diseases interfere with the sense of smell, including Alzheimer's disease, Parkinson's disease, multiple sclerosis, hypothyroidism, B_{12} deficiency, and even estrogen-positive breast carcinoma, a form of breast cancer. The loss of the ability to smell is a symptom that may help a doctor arrive at an accurate diagnosis. Despite the value of this testing, physicians rarely include it in physical examinations.

In our study involving law students, we used the University of Pennsylvania Smell Identification Test, which consists of a scratch-and-sniff 40-question test. Patients are asked to scratch one smell strip at a time, smell it, and identify the smell from the four choices given. Examples of the smells presented include pizza, lilac, menthol, and natural gas.

We asked the students to perform this test twice. The first time they took the 40-question test, we said, "Perform the test as if you couldn't smell, as if you were trying to get money from an insurance company." In other words we said, "Act like a faker." Then the second time they took the test, we told them to perform it "for real" and answer the questions honestly.

We anticipated that those who pretended they had lost their senses of smell would get one-quarter of the answers (10) correct by chance. Among University of Pennsylvania undergraduates, standardized tests revealed that participants would get about zero percent correct when they pretended to have smell loss, or up to one, two, or three correct. This suggests that they did not understand the random probabilities of scoring one of four correct, but rather, intentionally erred. The law students we tested were able to defeat the test. Even though they pretended they had smell loss, they did not fall within the malingering range but, rather, averaged approximately ten out of forty correct, despite having virtually all forty correct when they completed the test honestly. Thus, they were able to statistically predict how many they should miss and "accurately" falsified the results so that they averaged about ten out of forty correct. Therefore, law students were successfully able to beat the smell test and demonstrated themselves as being better liars than University of Pennsylvania undergraduates, or the population as a whole.

We don't know exactly why our law students were so good at deception and "gaming the test." They may have had a good understanding of statistics, and they've probably taken many standardized tests. They tend to be intelligent, and their group dynamics promote success, but these factors may or may not be important. However, it was clear that if anyone needed to find someone to lie for them, these law students would make a good choice!

As a parent, you can't necessarily prejudge your child as prone to deception based on an outgoing personality—or because she or he shows an interest in the law! But this is another piece of information that may alert you to your child's personality traits as she or he develops a moral code.

What Kind of a Lie Is It?

In order to help you detect a lie, it helps to understand varying kinds of lies you may encounter. In fact, as you go through the various stages of your child's development, you are likely to encounter certain kinds of deliberate or non-deliberate deception.

The unwitting lie

Regardless of personality, knowledge of the truth is also a component of a lie, or put another way, we have to know the truth in order to hide or distort it. Most of us make an honest, inadvertent mistake sometimes. To give an example from history, we recall that in a deposition that took place within weeks of his leaving office, President Reagan denied knowledge of certain elements in the Iran-Contra affair. On the surface and without other facts to inform our judgment, this denial could appear to be deliberate deception. But we later learned that he couldn't recall the names of his past Cabinet members, to give one example, because his Alzheimer's disease had progressed and his memory was unreliable. Thus, in order to lie, the difference between what's truth and what's false must be recognized. In these situations, we can't use body language and voice cues, for example, to detect a lie from our children.

For example, many teens go to parties where they believe the teen-host's parents will be present, and they tell you that in all sincerity. If that turns out not to be true, then that's an unwitting lie. If they tell you that knowing full well that the parents are out of town, then obviously that's deliberate deception. If they arrive at the party and stay, even though you've instructed them to leave unchaperoned situations, you have a different problem.

The self-convincing lie

On the other hand, in some situations, the child has convinced himself that his lie is true, and, in this situation, he may lie without a sense of guilt. He or she may look comfortable and confident, and exude a morally correct feeling. In a self-deception lie, the child has somehow convinced herself that the teen-host's parents were absolutely going to be home.

An unintentional lie, one in which the liar sincerely believes something that isn't true, represents one kind of lie that, as parents, we consider benign once we learn the facts. The self-convincing lie is not benign. We may have trouble detecting both, however.

The altruistic lie

Other types of lies—altruistic lies, lies of empathy, and lies of self-sacrifice for protection of a friend or relative—are associated with a moral position. It's unlike the so-called narcissistic lie that is defined by self-interest. Generally, no internal distress or anxiety is associated with this type of lie, although there are exceptions. In general, you may have trouble detecting this kind of lie.

You may be confused by now—most of us are. If your teenager is leaning toward sales, law, acting, or perhaps politics, or is an aspiring Mother Theresa or human rights leader, you may be perplexed by your child's ability to lie and your inability to accurately detect it. In other words, you may have an empathic, altruistic child, regardless of the field of endeavor, or you may have a natural liar on your hands.

What's the Payoff?

Because teens aren't quite adults, but are in a unique and discrete developmental stage, we need to look at what lying may mean to a teen. For example, we know that lying represents much more to teens in their still relatively powerless state than it does to adults, who by virtue of age have more personal power. When a teenager lies, it's as if they produce an alternate universe, one where what they want to be true becomes true and reality is suspended—the self-convincing lie. The universe they create liberates them and often produces a kind of euphoric state, especially when they know they've gotten away with something; the riskier the better. In fact, high-risk lying provides the thrill of a roller coaster in which the liar controls the tracks.

For a teenager, big lies feel good because they create an ideal state of being in which he or she maintains control. It's as if he or she is the president of his or her own company, the god of his or her own universe. All his or her narcissistic desires are met, and he or she is clearly superior to those who believed their lies. Not only does the teenage liar "get a carrot" by lying to his or her parents and demonstrating superiority over authority, but he or she avoids the "stick of punishment" from any perceived or actual wrong that the lie covers up. And, the more success teenage liars have, the more they lie. If they fool you once, they fool you twice, and they fool you forever. This manner of lying becomes ingrained in his interpersonal style of relating. What a payoff!

If they believe they can get away it, adolescents and younger children, too, will lie about anything they can get away with—from cleaning their rooms to hanging with friends, to going out, to studying. What's done, what's not done, what's happening, and what's not happening. As we've seen, they will lie about very big things, too, and once they get involved with chemical substances (or become sexually active, for example) they will tell bigger and bigger lies.

Breathing Free!

However, freedom may be the distinguishing factor between adult and teen lies. This stage of life brings frustration because teens still feel the yoke of parental authority. Parents are like the too intrusive, ever-present, micromanaging boss with power to track a teenager's every move. Parents always seem overbearing, even when issues of safety are concerned. Their kids don't see safety the same way. (This is another area in which the immature brain causes trouble.)

If they have the opportunity, kids will avoid answering simple questions about where they are going, what they are doing, and whom they're going to be with. They do this just because they believe they can. There may not be a practical payoff at all. These simple queries are reasonable to an adult, but teens may accuse parents of interrogating them. This reaction may sometimes lead to unnecessary lies—or simply withholding of information that's of no particular importance. This is part of a teen's "master of the universe" behavior.

Most lies teenagers tell can be broken down into:

- lies of omission and denial in order to avoid punishment for doing something they were prohibited from doing, or

- lies of commission, meaning they are trying to avoid responsibilities and tasks.

In some way, these lies relate to freedom, but they may also be training for adult behavior. Unfortunately for many parents, observant teenagers, having learned to lie from their parents, have also determined that it is usually easier to lie than to tell the truth. They don't actually accomplish tasks but, rather, simply say they have. This is the kind of lie that later turns into an adult's "padded" resumé. About one-third of resumés submitted in job applications include grossly falsified accomplishments, which goes beyond deft verbal manipulation. However, once a lie is accepted, it has a self-reinforcing mechanism that keeps the lie going, and the person continues to ignore the truth. It's the path of least resistance. I submit that most people would claim in all seriousness that their padded resumés actually only highlight legitimate accomplishments. (Oh, okay, you say no one *gave* you the title of supervisor, but you really did supervise five people—that's the way it worked out because you were better at your job than all those shirkers you had to work with.)

Do Teens Feel Guilt?

Just because teens can lie, that doesn't mean they will do so all the time about everything. If they've been guided and taught the basic concepts of right and wrong, then most teens do experience guilt. The anticipation of guilt may deter a teen from lying. Of course, if there's no motive or reason to lie, then teens, like adults, will choose the truth.

Also like adults, teens confront circumstances that present competing choices: tell the truth, avoid guilt, and feel good about one's self, or lie, avoid work and effort, and feel the twinge of guilt. The latter also sets up the concurrent risk of being discovered, and that means accepting shame, embarrassment, and external punishment for the lie.

What's a Parent to Do?

To shift the balance towards truthfulness in their teenagers, parents can adopt a number of strategies:

- They can act in a way to increase guilt, e.g., perhaps letting their teenager know in no uncertain terms, that his or her falsehoods caused a problem for another member of the family. This works well in a strong family system, where loyalty to siblings is strong.

- They can decrease work or effort expected or required for the truth, and sometimes that's as simple as saying something like, "So tell me about the drinking at the dance." (This assumes that you have a very good reason to believe drinking occurred. A statement that presents what you believe to be the truth can disarm even the sharpest teenager so the truth spills out—in many ways, this technique prevents the need to lie.)

- They can increase the chances of discovery of the falsehood, e.g., establishing very strict family rules and policies about checking in and verifying where the teen is. No law requires parents to establish a privacy policy. In other words, every-thing that involves your minor child, including what is said back and forth in emails with their friends, can be consid-ered your business.

- They can increase the punishment associated with discovery of the deception, e.g., upping the enforceable punishments. If a child was once grounded for a few days for coming in late, now make it a month. Nowadays, taking away com-puter use (other than for schoolwork) can be a perceived hardship to children.

It's essential that you use these approaches whenever a lie occurs; if you don't, then each successful lie serves as a breeding ground for additional lies. *So, even before you learn to detect a lie, establish what the consequences for lying will be.* That way you'll be fortified with a plan going forward.

As I advised in a previous chapter, the first step is to determine that a statement is a lie, and you can practice by listening and watch-ing both verbal and nonverbal communication. Let the previous list and illustrations guide you in detection.

Confronting the lie—or suspected lie

This is a critical stage in dealing with lies. Unfortunately, parents may back out at this stage. They may lose their nerve or begin to doubt their own evaluation of the situation at hand. Sometimes, other motivations and emotions cloud their judgment. Maybe they're tired from their own long days, or they don't want to turn another evening into a battle. More seriously, they may have crises of confidence and have all but given up. Or they may be in denial and prefer to believe that the lie they've exposed may not be so important after all. I urge you to resist your own temptation to take the path of least resistance. *Confront the lie! And then move on from there.*

Maximizing guilt

Since most lying occurs without external punishment (because it may go undetected), self-punishment by inducing guilt is the tool of choice to prevent lying. Growing up in a Jewish household, I know that guilt is liberally applied, like peanut butter and jelly. A Jewish mother (literal or figurative!) and guilt are the backbone—the entire skeleton for that matter—of the childhood and teenage years, even on into adulthood.

Obviously, one can carry this to an extreme, and I certainly don't suggest that parents foster guilt over every little thing. But the purpose of guilt is to inhibit unacceptable behavior until the concepts of right and wrong are instilled. In today's language, perhaps our teenagers will relate to and accept the concepts of responsibility and accountability. But it's time to explain the value of this. It's a myth that feeling guilt or feeling bad about doing something wrong is psychologically harmful. A child who doesn't feel guilt is set up to develop sociopathy, an anti-social personality.

In adult life, many mistakes are avoided by anticipating guilty feelings. If we know we must take responsibility for actions or situations, then we're more likely to demand the best from ourselves. Likewise, holding our children accountable for their actions makes them consider and weigh their choices. They are less likely to act out in destructive ways when they know we're paying attention and will call them on it.

By becoming an expert in instilling guilt in her children, the literal or proverbial Jewish mother controls their behavior, even when she's not present. The fear of guilt alone is enough to prevent the behavior. While this doesn't necessarily strengthen the child-mother bond, it does keep teens' rebellious instincts under control so they become "good boys and girls." And that means avoiding alcohol, crime, and all manner of mayhem. It also induces acceptance of maternal desires to embrace the norms of society and socially approved roles as good citizen and family member.

After decades of working with troubled families, I've come to believe that guiltless parenting on the part of one or two parents (or even more, if we count parents in blended families) often fosters a child's lack of a good moral compass, and we can't afford to let that happen. The age of permissiveness is over. Rather than dividing children and parents, setting standards and expecting children to meet them promotes trust, not hostility. The unhappiest children are those who don't feel valued and who are left to fend for themselves.

Obviously, building a child's moral compass is a big challenge for all parents, but especially for single mothers, who must instill this constructive guilt in their children while simultaneously building a maternal-child bond of unconditional acceptance. Two parents can divide the roles, i.e., the father can lean toward being the accepting parent, while the mother plays the guilt-producing role, or vice-versa, of course.

While single-parent families face special challenges, in a family without a stable parent or a temporary parent, as in a foster home, then no one assumes either role. This is why some children are predisposed to a moral code that accepts lying and may develop sociopathic behavior or antisocial personality disorder.

So what's the best way to instill guilt for lying? In brief, we need to express disappointment while maintaining unconditional love for the child. Children, even older teens, want to please their parents. Knowing that their parents are unhappy operates as a force that often changes the way kids behave. The change is designed to enhance happiness in the caregivers. But, in order to maximize guilt, it must be instilled at each opportunity when a lie occurs.

The special case of the altruistic lie

When my daughter Marissa, now in high school, was a fourth grader, she made a kiln-hardened clay turtle as a gift to my wife and me. It was on display like a priceless, invaluable possession on our hallway dresser. My wife and I were not pleased to discover it smashed to pieces, and to see our nine-year-old daughter, Camryn, with a guilty expression. She had obviously accidentally broken the turtle while playing with her younger brother, Noah. Staring straight at Camryn, I asked who had done this deed. Camryn refused to say she broke the turtle.

When confronted with a situation like this, we can convert the lie to the truth through one of three mechanisms: (1) increasing the risk of being caught, (2) increasing the punishment for lying, and (3) reducing the adverse impact of telling the truth. These approaches are common and routinely used in the criminal justice system. Police officers will bluff by telling a suspect that damaging evidence against them exists or will threaten the suspect with a long sentence if convicted or negotiate a reduced sentence for a guilty plea.

Applying these same interrogative approaches to Camryn, I enhanced her stress level by evoking the belief that she was already caught at the lie. "Camryn," I said, "admit that you broke this turtle. I can see by the smirk on your face that you're not being honest."

This approach takes advantage of the psychological pressures to reveal the truth. My insistence that she admit the truth added to the pressure, and, with this, it lifted the burden of guilt associated with telling the lie. This is similar to the relief experienced with legal and religious confessions. It's also like the relief experienced when patients divulge their innermost secrets and fantasies during psychotherapy.

In *A Tale of Two Cities*, Charles Dickens wrote that all humanity travels through life with unrevealed secrets, that we take to our graves. By providing the enticement and pressure to force revelation of these secrets, the weight of carrying this burden is relieved and the liar feels uplifted. Literature is filled with examples of the burden of guilt that destroys a person, and the nearly euphoric relief that can occur when the lie is released and confession is complete.

Informing Camryn that I knew the truth and telling her that her smirking had been the element that led to her being caught did, in effect, increase the risk of being caught, and she knew this in her own mind. So, from her viewpoint, she was as good as caught, which left her with the choice to either dig in further and continue the lie or admit the lie and move forward. Sometimes a stubborn streak leads a person, child, or adult, to become more committed to the lie and dig in deeper. In that case, parents (and other "interrogators") must bring on additional pressure.

As it happened, my daughter Camryn showed this stubborn streak and chose to dig in. I was forced to go to the second level of increasing the punishment for lying.

Camryn was sent to her room as a punishment. The enclosed and isolated physical space of a child's room is the family equivalent of solitary confinement. As parents, the punishments that we are able to mete out are limited. Short of laying hands on the child (which I would recommend only as a last resort), the psychological trauma of a time-out, even in the teenage years, has strong advantages. By being separated and put into a room where he is alone, the child recognizes he has been isolated from the rest of the society of the family. Furthermore, he is removed from the creature comforts of food and entertainment (such as a favorite TV program or family movie night), which is why it is important that the child does not have a computer or television in his room. During this time of isolation, he either can consider the implications of his action and/or spend time doing productive things such as reading.

In a sense, we meted out the punishment without the admission of the lie. Everything pointed to the facts, and we were confident in our confrontation. Our intention was, at some point, to probe for understanding of what she did wrong and what change she might make in the future. However, Camryn continued to deny that she had done it, despite threats of more time-outs unless she admitted doing it.

Fear of losing face may come into play as well. In this situation involving Camryn, it seemed as if she dug in to defend an elaborate, multi-layered lie. We see this often with kids. Admitting one component of the lie unravels the whole scheme. However, in this case, Camryn, after a couple of forced time-outs, admitted that she had broken the turtle and lied about it.

Oops—The System Isn't Perfect!

Later that night, before bed, my youngest son, Noah, approached me, brimming with guilt, since he'd actually broken the turtle. Out of an altruistic spirit, his older sister had taken the blame. In this mini-family drama, Noah displayed the guilt of having someone else take the blame, and his discomfort with seeing his sister being punished tipped the scale. He confessed because he couldn't go to bed as he was so bothered by what had taken place. No doubt, having the truth come out lifted a burden from him.

Those who tell altruistic lies don't experience the guilt of having violated the social norm of telling the truth, because their lies are "good" lies. On one hand, Camryn had to live with the disapproval of her parents. On the other hand, she was learning the differences of the so-called altruistic lie. Most of the time, like a seesaw, there is a balance between the discomfort of having told a lie and the perceived social reward or sense of higher purpose associated with telling the altruistic lie. This applies to the lies of social lubrication, where we spare another person's feelings or try to make another person feel better. That's a different kind of lie than taking the blame for someone else, because it has the potential to harm the family system or encourage an unhealthy selflessness. In children, the altruism may also turn negative. I'm sure that one day, Camryn will be sure to remind Noah of the time "she took the rap" for him—most siblings can't resist the opportunity to tease in that way.

When Parents Make Mistakes

To a large degree, the ability to detect a lie depends upon the motivation of the liar. In my experience with my daughter Camryn, I was inaccurate in detecting the lie because I let the circumstantial evidence lead me down the path of presumption of guilt until proven otherwise. I'd made up my mind that she lied before she was able to extricate herself from my preconceived notion. Admittedly, these kinds of errors can drive a wedge in the parent-child relationship. Camryn wasn't an adolescent, so we had to go through a process of reviewing the incident and letting her know we now understood the truth.

Fortunately, by the time they become teenagers, your kids already know you are not perfect and are capable of making many mistakes. Should you inadvertently inaccurately accuse your child of lying, she will just chalk this up to her parent being inept and incompetent. If this happens often, however, then her trust in you could erode. And she will realize that if you misperceive the truth for a lie, then she can probably reverse it and may have a greater chance of lying so that you will be unaware of the truth.

Still, regardless of the mistake I made in this case, I believe that confronting the lie is critical. If you don't confront each and every lie, children will get better at lying and realize that they can lie succesfully. They may lose respect for your authority as a parent—and you need that respect in order to be an effective parent.

In order to accurately detect and confront the lie, it is important that you are not directed away from the methods of detecting whether or not a lie occurred. You also don't want to be misled by the contents of the lie but, rather, look at the verbal and nonverbal signs your child is giving you. If I had done that more carefully with Camryn, I would not have misjudged her as lying.

Accepting Full Responsibility

By taking responsibility for a lie, a child can be held accountable for future lies. My son Jack knocked over a plate of cookies in the kitchen, and when confronted, he said that the cookies fell down when he had walked near them. After pressing him, though, he admitted that he was responsible for knocking the plate over, as opposed to the cookies spontaneously falling off the counter just as he walked by.

As we see over and over, if children are not taught to assume responsibility, their behavior won't change. By forcing responsibility, children recognize that they are the agents that control what they do. In other words, they have choices and can take action. Too many adults were given the impression as children that life is a series of events that happens to us, and that we don't have any responsibility for. Accidents, for example, may fall into this category. Some adults understand that safety measures, such as using protective items like seat belts and cycling helmets, are part of taking responsibility for their own well-being. That doesn't mean that things can't go wrong, but it does mean they are taking charge of what is within their control. This attitude applies to their words.

Let's face it, it's easier not to confront the lie and force responsibility, because it will often mean butting heads, so to speak, and that means discomfort all around. But not confronting the lie emboldens the liar and encourages further lying. Why not lie in the future if they can get away it and won't be held responsible?

Consequences for a Lie

While the punishment might vary from a scolding or a time-out or physical restraint (for young children) to taking away a range of privileges (for older children), it's essential that the liar be punished. Without that step, the child will learn that it is okay to lie because there will never be consequences for it. On the other hand, resist the temptation to over-punish, which will cause the child to dissociate himself from you and rebel. In a later chapter, we'll discuss the top lies and possible appropriate consequences. But, first, we'll address an age-old problem all teenagers and parents face.

Chapter 7

Is Teen Privacy Overrated?

When our kids are very young, we tend to spend time interacting in both playful and care-giving ways. For example, we sing to babies as we change their diapers and we play games with toddlers as we teach them the alphabet or to count their fingers. During this process, we're setting limits and establishing ourselves as the authority figures in their world. They can count on us to meet their needs, and we feel free to have fun with our children, while also being firm about our rules and values as we teach them the ways of the world.

We also use these years to teach our children to take increasing responsibility for various elements in their lives and to encourage their growing independence. However, as our children enter their teen years, it may be tempting to change our behavior and turn our children into companions and friends.

While we always want to enjoy our teenagers as much as possible, we run the risk of abdicating our parental authority if we blur the line between parent and child. Once relinquished, parental authority can be difficult to get back. This tendency to blur the lines often comes in an effort to appease a sullen or angry teen. Or the teenager has taken to talking about how embarrassing it is to be around you—a natural phase, by the way. Perhaps he or she is determined to resist your rules and claims to be the only boy or girl who can't stay out after midnight or who doesn't have his or her own car or computer.

This stage, marked by extreme unhappiness with your boundaries and rules, can be very difficult. However, it's better to have your son "die of embarrassment" than die in an auto accident while driving under the influence. Better to have your daughter furious because you keep track of her Internet activity than end up being stalked (or worse) by a predator. Don't believe all the talk about how cool other parents are. Most of the time it isn't true, and if these parents are so cool, they may be acting more like friends than parents.

Parents and teenagers can enjoy mutual activities and hobbies, but the balance of authority should remain weighted on the parents' side. There will be plenty of time after the teen years are over to shift the balance toward an enjoyable, equal relationship with your adult children. Eventually, in those years, your children will assert themselves and remind you that they are adults, and their claim will be legitimate. However, if they try this "I'm an adult" argument when they're 15 or even 17, then you can remind them who's in charge.

One way in which they will surely test your authority involves privacy, including the degree of privacy they expect in your home.

Do Teens Have a Right to Privacy?

When it comes to adolescents and their need for or right to privacy, we first must ask why we believe, as many of us do, that it's an issue in the first place. For many of us raised at a time when we and our friends roamed more freely in our environment, independence and privacy went together in ongoing and incremental steps. When I was an adolescent, most parents believed that teenagers were entitled to some degree of privacy. They treated it as an expanding privilege: the older we were and the more self-care and responsibility we took on, the more privacy we earned.

Times change. The path to earning privacy was forged in a time before almost every teenager owned a phone and probably a computer, too. Given the way many of us grew up, privacy was hard to come by. The phone was in the kitchen or the entry hall, and the family home had one, maybe two bathrooms, and at least two kids shared each bedroom. In fact, one of the privileges of advancing through the teen years may have involved being allowed to have a room of one's own, or at least a make-shift space in the basement or garage. A private phone line may have been a special privilege.

Obviously, many teenagers still share bedrooms and bathrooms, but, in our society, moving into larger homes with more rooms and opportunities to be alone is an ongoing trend. This has pros and cons, because while it's pleasant to spread out and have quiet and privacy when we feel the need for it, it can also cut into family cohesiveness and allow kids too much privacy.

Let's challenge some of the basic assumptions about modern teen life. For example, if it's true that the computer represents one of the biggest threats to our children's wellbeing and even safety, why do we let teens isolate themselves for hours at a time in their rooms with their computers and internet connections? If we believe television contains unwholesome programming, even during so-called primetime, family viewing hours, then why do we allow children to have TVs in their rooms? Today's adolescents may also have their own cars or have friends with cars, and that presents additional issues to monitor, including increased occasions to lie.

Between TV, text messaging, and online capabilities that offer something new every day, our children can move freely in the world without leaving home. Even the most conscientious parents may have trouble keeping track of their kids' activities. This is complicated by the confusion over what is and is not "your business." If we leave this up to our kids, we would know very little about them!

Confronting Change

At one time, I assumed that I'd take an egalitarian approach to privacy and even values issues. I harkened back to my own childhood, when, as pre-teens and teens, our parents were fairly confident about our safety in the world. My friends and I rode our bikes or walked to school and took public transportation and commuter trains from our suburb into downtown Chicago.

Before I actually had children, I looked forward to the day when my future kids could explore the world on their own too. But several things have changed. First, concerns about our children's safety have altered the way we live, and today many children never ride their bikes or walk to school. They board school buses or are driven by their parents. In my children's school district, a mounted camera in the bus even monitors them as a deterrent to misbehavior, and if a fight breaks out or bullying goes on, the camera picks it up. In addition, children of all ages are confronted with many more temptations at earlier ages than in the past. When I was child in elementary school, drug dealers were shadowy figures that we believed lurked in alleys in city neighborhoods. Today, we know that no community is without its share of drug dealers, and high school students don't necessarily need to drive into the city to make their deals. Alcohol isn't that hard to get.

We had fewer occasions to be teased or tempted with sexually graphic and even suggestive material. While it's true that standards began to drop in the 1970s and boundaries have continued to change, we haven't bottomed out. Today's typical sitcom is at the very least suggestive and usually crude as well. In addition, the amount of media available on the Internet and cable TV has increased exposure to inappropriate material. Even typical ads in magazines young people read are sexier and encourage young people to adopt an adult style of dress and speech.

I was motivated to study lying and apply what I'd learned to adolescents at least in part because of my experiences as a physician with so many patients with one or more addictions who made so many poor life choices as young people that carried long-term consequences. All served as warning signs about our unfettered young people, often drifting along without goals or aims or a sense of belonging to a family or society. Deception is almost always a theme in the lives of those who have fallen into addiction or other destructive behavior.

I saw mounting evidence of what happens when risk-taking teenagers are given too much freedom and their needs are neglected in the name of privacy. Sometimes it's by default, in that no one was paying much attention to what these young people were up to. They had loose curfews at best, and they lacked a strong adult willing or able to effectively enforce the rules. This decline in monitoring or guiding teens cuts across socioeconomic lines. Kids with luxury cars and plenty of money in their pockets can aimlessly drift into trouble every bit as quickly as the child who must scratch for survival in declining neighborhoods or rural communities.

My previous attitudes about privacy changed as I saw the shift in predominant influences on our children. As a result, my wife and I have adapted our views of independence and privacy to *current* conditions, not an idealized past. I believe some strategies and family policies we've adopted may help you as well, so I'm passing them on.

Deception and Privacy

When my wife and I reevaluated the concept of teens and privacy, we saw many opportunities to provide a wholesome, safe environment for our children, while at the same time reducing the occasions for deception and outright lies. In other words, we keep such close tabs on our pre-teens and teenagers that the natural sources of temptation are thwarted. In addition, the rules you create contribute to the larger picture of what kind of family unit you desire.

Computers, friend or danger zone?

Today, when even preschoolers can operate so many gadgets, including computers, it's worthwhile to monitor your children's technological activities right from the start. That may be difficult if you feel that a child should have a computer in his or her room. My wife and I decided against that. The computers, which are really just an extension of television, are kept out in the open in common areas, and we limit time spent on them. Computer research for school and doing homework are legitimate reasons for kids to be on the computer. If they're going to play computer games you allow or visit web sites related to special interests, they can also do that out in the open.

The dangers involved in predatory behavior are reason enough to monitor your teenager's computer time. The computer is a portal for predators. You would never allow your child to open the door to strangers and invite them into your house, but that's exactly what can happen when your child engages in hours of free and unquestioned computer use.

If you ask your children what web sites they regularly visit, do you think they'll admit to spending hours on celebrity gossip sites or posting pictures of themselves on each other's MySpace pages? Will they tell you about the chat rooms they visit? Ask yourself right now if you are aware of any pictures of your children posted anywhere on the Internet.

Even with the computer out in the open, regularly check the browser history in front of your child. Keep track of the sites he or she is visiting; make the rules clear and let your child know you're enforcing them. If, like my son Jack, your child wants to check the latest sports scores, he or she can do that after he or she has shown you his or her finished homework assignments.

The issue of teenagers and the time they spend on the Internet is not trivial. According to research conducted by the Pew Internet and American Life Project, 73% (more than 17 million) of teenagers use the Internet and consider it a major part of their lives. Teenage blogging has become a common pastime for about *4 million* teens (mostly girls); these young people may discuss all kinds of personal issues on their blogs, not really understanding that what they write can be accessed by virtually anyone. These young teens show their naiveté when they demand privacy from you, but fail to grasp the extent to which online "diaries" expose their lives to strangers—and predators.

If you discover that your child has set up a blog, then you may learn things about your child that will disturb you; you may also read different versions of the stories they have told you about school, boyfriends, parties, and so on. Parents who are just coming to the realization that their kids are lying should check their children's Internet presence. Except for completing class assignments, computer use should be considered a privilege that can be revoked at any time. I'd put a quick stop to a blog. They are potentially dangerous for young teens and a waste of time. I would discourage your college-age children from blogging on MySpace or a similar site, too, simply because their time is better spent in other ways. Even writing skills are known to be substandard on blogs and in social sites. If they insist, then they can engage in these things when they're off on their own. (Children who show interest in creative writing can join the staff of the school newspaper or literary magazine, or join real-world—as opposed to Internet—literary clubs.) All these online activities cut into face-to-face social interactions with friends and siblings. In addition, the time spent online also allows teens, who may be moody and often feeling sad, too much opportunity to retreat into a narrow and unreal (in many ways) world. Devoid of adult supervision, this virtual world offers an alternative, but it's a false, potentially dangerous, all-consuming life that becomes a detriment to their psychological development. Therefore, you have to provide it by monitoring all online activity.

Television time

A friend of mine complained that her son lied about doing his homework. She'd knock on his door and when she'd open it, the TV screen would be flickering off. "He's watching TV while he does math homework or writes history papers on the computer," she said. "Then he tries to cover it up and denies it when I confront him." This mother didn't know what to do and asked me how we handled this situation in our home.

First, I see no reason for children to have television sets in their rooms. Eliminate the TV, and you eliminate the occasion to lie about watching it while doing homework! Second, even if you allow your child to have her own TV, you can, for example, make a house rule that the bedroom door must be kept open while she's doing homework or reading.

We don't allow our children to have their own TVs for much the same reason that we don't allow them to have their own computers. Studies show that children with TVs in their rooms do less reading than those who don't have TVs. Too much television also leads to greater incidence of childhood obesity. Magazine and television reports lament all the time adults and children spend watching TV, but then we keep buying more televisions.

At one time, the teenagers may have wasted a few hours watching some lame programs on a handful of network channels. But the combination of cable TV (even non-premium channels) and significantly lower decency standards mean that your children can find unending images of sex and violence, and hear offensive language. Watching TV in isolation sets up an occasion to lie about what programs your child watches and when.

As an aside, some of the so-called family-hour dramas show incredibly unhealthy behavior, such as regular drinking and premarital sex among high school students. That's bad enough, but these behaviors are treated as normal, rarely questioned unless some problem like a DUI or a pregnancy occurs. The issue raised revolves around the teenager not handling the activity well. These programs rarely promote the firm idea that teens shouldn't be drinking and having sex in the first place.

Cell phones and text messaging

For various reasons, parents may want their children to have cell phones. This is another recent trend and usually involves safety concerns, such as insuring the ability to communicate with their children at any time. It also seems related to the phenomenon of "chauffeur parents," those who spend considerable time on the road taking their kids to school and to various activities.

Having instant access to our children is one thing; allowing our children to use their phones to text message their friends is another. Here, too, my wife and I have set our own policy. Our 15-year-old daughter, Marissa, has a cell phone, but no text messaging capability. Our primary reason is that text messaging is one of the biggest time-wasting activities known to man! It has no legitimate useful purpose for a teenager and, like roaming the Internet or spending endless hours alone watching TV, cuts into family time.

What Are They Hiding?

Obviously, teenagers have reached the age at which they are entitled to certain kinds of privacy, such as bathing and dressing alone. We don't have a need to eavesdrop on every phone call or casually read their diaries without cause. However, what looks like a demand for privacy may be a cover for secrecy—and a desire to sneak around the rules of your household.

If you limit the in-house opportunities to lie—TV, phones, and computers—you may find yourself in a stronger position overall. Rarely have I heard of a parent rifling through a child's room or dresser drawers or closet without cause. Snooping for snooping's sake never plays well. Curiosity about what an otherwise trusted teenager is writing about in a journal, for example, will be viewed as a violation of trust. But, while you want to respect your teens' belongings, you also want to make sure that your children understand that nothing is 100% off limits to you as a parent. If you believe they are lying to you, their safety is threatened, or their well-being is at stake, you have the right to investigate.

Chapter 8

What Interferes with Telling and Learning the Truth?

Even the best intentions can be thwarted when it comes to establishing an atmosphere where telling the truth is second nature—and the norm for everyone in the family. For example, certain conditions, such as depression or attention deficit disorder (ADD), affect the course of a child's development and, for various reasons, may interfere with an honest and open attitude toward parents. Just as important, parents may waver in their resolve to learn the truth and create an atmosphere where honesty prevails.

More than any other factor, your intention and determination to uncover the truth about a situation greatly influences the outcome. This is the single most important factor your children must understand as you move forward to improve your ability to both detect deception and encourage truth-telling. Before we examine what can go wrong with teenagers, let's look at parents' attitudes.

Family Harmony—Is It a Myth?

Too often parents make decisions based on the desire to keep the peace and maintain family harmony. Because of nostalgia, which is a yearning for an idealized past, many parents put a high value on creating a family life similar to the fictional version they saw on *Leave It to Beaver*. In this idealized world, parents are always around to give wise counsel, and, if Wally or the Beaver break the rules, the boys eventually act contrite, the lesson is learned, and the story returns to light comedy. Or in Mayberry U.S.A., the biggest problem is finding time for Andy to take Opie fishing. Life was never that simple then, and we are certainly aware that it's not that simple now.

In the quest for that kind of life, however, parents often allow too many small deceptions and lies of omission to slide, as if letting something pass will make it go away. We do this for many reasons, including:

The desire to avoid unpleasantness in our households

My wife and I find ourselves demanding (again and again) to know who left food out on the kitchen counter. We have four possible culprits. True, it would be easier to just clear away the open containers of milk and the cereal boxes from the counter ourselves rather than nag the kids to follow the rules and clean up after themselves. However, we believe we must turn these small things into occasions to demonstrate that denials—lies—are unacceptable at any age, even in regards to these seemingly minor infractions. Besides, being allowed to leave messes and not clean up after themselves sends a poor message. If parents turn into their children's servants, then family harmony is undermined anyway, not to mention that then these young adults will not internalize a sense of responsibility.

Harmony is important, but your children's character develop-ment and safety are more important. An overly tranquil environ-ment may mean that trouble is simmering underneath, and it will surely boil over into the teenage years. Making sure your children tell the truth when young sets the tone for their middle-childhood and teenage years. Like adults, children are creatures of habit and resist change. Consistency and predictability help you maintain a degree of peace and harmony, but harmony alone shouldn't be the goal.

We fear being called nags
"Lighten up, Dad," or, "I said I'd clean my room before dinner; quit nagging." Parents hear this kind of complaint all the time. Our teens love to tune us out. But there are worse things than being called a nag. If we start identifying with our kids' opinions of us, we run the risk of backing off. We let the chores go undone, we give up on checking homework, or we take care of things that the kids are old enough to do for themselves, all of which send the message that we can be manipulated to back down.

Calling us nags is nothing more than manipulation. The "get off my back" attitude may seem benign when it comes to a 10-year-old's undone chores, but it's not so benign when your 16-year-old wants to avoid telling you where she went after school without your knowledge. All in all, being called a nag may mean that you're being conscientious—it's actually a compliment.

We tire of the same old issues
With all the pressures of day-to-day work and raising one or more children, we may be tempted to back away from confrontation. Or perhaps we feel overwhelmed by the demands on us as parents. Like the little Dutch boy with his finger plugging the hole in the dike,

we seem to always be holding back trouble and worried that more holes will appear.

Well, no one said raising kids would be easy. One of the most difficult day-to-day challenges is maintaining the standards you set in your home. Follow-through, especially when parents are worn out, is difficult, but children try our patience in order to wear us down. The fastest way to eliminate some of these same old issues is to handle them consistently. If you strictly enforce curfew or monitor the computer or check that your teenagers have cleaned their rooms or finished their homework, then these standards and rules become part of the household routine. Of course, this process can be very tiring, but consistent results demand consistent efforts.

We prematurely try to be pals to our teens

Too many parents surrender their roles as parents because they fear that their children will dislike them. As I said earlier, it's not your role to be a friend or pal, and it's not important that your teenagers like you. Some parents have a difficult time accepting the shift from dealing with dependent and amusing young children to adolescents who sometimes reject them. Research shows, however, that teenagers respect parents who hold firm to the rules and boundaries. When expectations get fuzzy, then the teens will push until they reach a boundary, because they want the security of their parents' protection and attention. This is part of the confusion. Your teen may reject you on the one hand, while on the other hand feeling deep relief that you are overriding her bad judgment and forbidding potentially harmful activities.

Complications and Detours

You may be coping with problems different from those we typically associate with the rebellious teenage years. While we expect a degree of confusion and "growing pains" in the transition from children to young adults, certain conditions and difficulties may interfere and lead to troublesome behavior.

Sociopathy in teens

Unfortunately, some children develop a sociopathic personality, a true psychological disorder. (The causes of sociopathy aren't clear.) These individuals may be unable to distinguish right from wrong, or they may understand the concepts but are indifferent to right and wrong, and lack a well-developed conscience, meaning that they are incapable of experiencing guilt and remorse.

The sociopathic personality begins developing early, but it may become fully apparent during the teenage years. Throughout their children's early and middle years, parents must watch for certain signs of this disorder, including patterns of bullying behavior, cruelty to animals, lying about big things and issues of no consequence. Sociopaths often make up tall tales for no particular reason other than their own ego gratification. These are serious behavioral patterns that point to major problems.

Teens exhibiting signs of sociopathic personality disorder may engage in shoplifting, for example, and may start skipping school and become chronic truants. This is particularly true since a substantial amount of teen shoplifting takes place in affluent communities, and the items stolen are not linked to basic needs but reflect a desire for material things. Carried to its logical end, we see the extreme of this sociopathic behavior in gang or organized crime activities, which show no regard for laws that govern all of us. Harming bystanders in drive-by shootings, for example, can only occur in an atmosphere in which the lives of other people, except for one's own family and friends, are disregarded. These misplaced loyalties tend to become ingrained by the teenage years, which is why teens may find it difficult to leave street gangs. Developmentally, the teenage years tend to embolden young people to act on their defiant and self-centered impulses, and I urge you to watch for early signs of this personality disorder.

Shoplifting tends to be a repetitive crime, seldom, if ever, based on need. Sociopathic personality types tend to be attracted to a crime like shoplifting because it gives them a thrill—a rush. They feel satisfaction, even pride, in getting away with it. However, shoplifting is also something kids may try in groups, and it may be a way of acting out, pushing a boundary.

If your child is caught shoplifting, it is unlikely that it's the first time he or she has done it. Most kids who steal tend to repeat the act. The exception would involve a child accepting a dare in the heat of the moment, for example. This is the time to probe deeply into what led to committing the crime. It may be that your teenager is hanging out with new and, to you at least, unlikely friends. This is the time to nip in the bud this new found bravado and defiance of what are long-standing values and rules.

If you see signs of sociopathic personality disorder at any point in your child's development, be aggressive in taking stock and seeking help. You may note that your seven- or eight-year-old isn't adopting your sense of right and wrong and doesn't appear to feel guilt or shame over breaking a rule or getting caught at something like cheating in school. In this situation, I recommend discussing your concerns with your pediatrician, who can refer you to appropriate help. If you have noticed these signs for awhile and now your child is entering adolescence, then you'll need to be even more aggressive in seeking help.

Is every incident of shoplifting, for example, a sign that your child is a sociopath? The answer is a conditional no. Some teenagers go through a stage in which they feign indifference to right and wrong. It's part of their attempt to separate from you. Rejecting basic values may be part of an ill-conceived declaration of independence. If you've noticed recent changes in your teenager and then an incident of shoplifting is exposed, you have a chance to stop and reverse the course. It's possible that they are showing false sociopathic personality traits. For example, parents usually claim that their otherwise well-behaved children wouldn't have stolen from the store if they hadn't become involved with "the wrong crowd." Or bullying incidents may result from unwisely following a misguided leader.

It is possible to distinguish the true sociopath from the newly emboldened teen, who is temporarily taking the wrong path, when you see what carries over from one environment to another. If your child goes to a new school, for example, and the problem is corrected, then this behavior was a fluke of some kind. However, a child with a sociopathic personality disorder will engage in the same behavior in the new school.

Attention deficit disorder (ADD), attention deficit hyperactivity disorder (ADHD), and learning disabilities

Debates about attention deficit disorders, with or without the hyperactivity factor, are ongoing in the medical world and among parents looking for information. If you're a parent with questions or are confused about symptoms your child displays, you are a not alone. ADD and ADHD are perplexing conditions. You probably wonder if your child's behavioral and academic issues can be treated with the correct medication. Since I don't know your child's specific medical, developmental, or behavioral history, I can't make a diagnosis or advise you about appropriate treatment, except to urge you to seek help and not live on hope that these problems will simply vanish one day.

In addition, these conditions or the presence of a learning disability does not mean that your child will have a greater tendency to lie. However, problems may develop if the child isn't adequately diagnosed, monitored, and treated, because academic performance and following rules both at home and in school are very difficult for many children with these disorders. Children who are singled out for teasing because they have trouble with certain learning tasks or who can't adjust to typical classroom expectations may act out, and their unhappiness and maladjustment may be what leads to deceptive behavior. They often show poor impulse control, and some children with behavioral and learning problems may try to cheat in school or falsify their school papers and report cards.

It's important to understand that attention deficit disorders and learning disabilities are treatable conditions. Unfortunately, some people still insist that lack of discipline or "soft" parenting causes certain behavioral problems, thereby failing to appreciate how difficult the learning process becomes when these problems go unrecognized. However, ADD essentially involves decreased activity in the part of the brain that controls concentration, which influences attention span. ADHD adds the element of excessive energy and activity. Learning disabilities, such as the perceptual difficulty dyslexia, often occur with ADD/ADHD, further complicating a child's ability to adjust to standard teaching methods.

It's notable that in the U.S., the incidence of ADHD is 10 to 1, boys to girls, making this appear to be a primarily male disease. On the other hand, in the United Kingdom (U.K.), the incidence is equally distributed, 1 to 1, boys to girls. Why so great a difference? Well, in the U.K., boys start school a year later than girls do. While this might seem odd, it makes sense, because it takes longer for boys' brains to mature, and this is why we see a disparity between boys and girls in ADHD.

In addition, boys tend to process information in a physical, experiential manner, whereas girls tend to process information in a cognitive, verbal manner. That's why girls generally have better verbal skills than boys do early in life. These differences tend to even out as both sexes progress through childhood. Given this disparity of developmental rates, we subject our male children to demands in early childhood that many are unable to fulfill. This induces pathology in the form of ADHD-type behavior, and these boys act out in different ways, including aggressive behavior in school, bullying, lying, and so on.

The challenge for parents of children with ADD/ADHD or learning disabilities involves finding the right school environment in which the child can best learn. Schools tend to be competitive settings, and poor performance may damage such a child's self-image and result in a defiant attitude and attention seeking. These children are often so miserable in school that their frustration level gets them into trouble. Kids with chronic learning/behavioral problems tend to lie as a coping mechanism, and they are prime candidates for delinquency and dropping out of school. It's no accident that many men and women in our prison system show evidence of undiagnosed learning disabilities and ADD. On the other hand, many highly successful individuals have achieved their goals in spite of their learning disabilities and attention disorders.

Children with ADD or a related condition may believe the myth that they aren't as smart as everyone else. However, their intelligence levels fall in the normal range. Seeking help to obtain proper diagnosis and treatment can break the cycle, and provide the opportunity for the child to progress through school and develop a healthy self-image.

Childhood and adolescent depression

We see depression, a widespread mood disorder, among individuals of all ages, including children. Bipolar disorder is a related condition, and, although it's less common, it can lead to careless, impulsive behavior in young people, especially those attracted to high-risk activities. Unfortunately, in children and adolescents, depression may be written off as simply a case of the blues or typical teenage moodiness. For many centuries, depression deeply affected millions of individuals who suffered without effective remedies to relieve their symptoms. Even in the last century, mild and moderate depression often went undiagnosed; today, however, we have many treatment options. We also recognize that depression in adolescents is common, and should not be confused with normal sadness, or sullen or melancholy behavior.

Fortunately, we now understand depression as a disease with many possible physical and psychological symptoms, including fatigue, headaches, anxiety, and exaggerated symptoms of stress. In teenagers, we may see eating disorders and phobias develop, along with suicidal thoughts and outbursts of temper. Teens suffering from depression may swing from being sad to angry and, like adults, may have crying spells that can't be linked to a cause. While we still have many unanswered questions about depression, it tends to run in families, so there is a genetic component.

Depression involves the imbalance or insufficient production of certain brain chemicals, or neurotransmitters. The key neurotransmitters are serotonin, which regulates mood and sleep, norepinephrine, which is involved in our energy levels, and dopamine, which is involved in our overall sense of well-being and also decreases our sensitivity to pain. Antidepressant medications are designed to correct these imbalances and elevate low levels of these key neurotransmitters.

To clarify, it's important to know that depression itself is not linked to dishonest behavior. However, young people suffering from depression may lie about what they eat, or how much or how well they sleep, for example. They may avoid responsibility and prefer to isolate themselves. Behavioral changes in your teenager may be linked to depression. For example, if your gregarious child is spending time alone in her room and loses interest in siblings or school, then it makes sense to investigate the reasons behind the change.

It's generally believed that depression is a biologically-based disorder. However, trauma or loss may trigger depression in some cases. Family difficulties, such as divorce or the death of a parent, may be an underlying cause of depression. A teenager may become preoccupied with a girlfriend or boyfriend or other troubles with friends. When they can't shake off the disappointment, anger, or feelings of loss, then they may be at risk of developing depression.

During periods of greater stress, your child is at higher risk to self-medicate, that is, find relief in drugs, alcohol, or cigarettes. Nicotine has a subtle effect on the brain that may give the user a temporary sense of calm or contentment. While this relief is short-lived, the child may repeat the behavior, thereby setting up a situation in which lying becomes necessary in order to keep using the substance. Soon, a full-blown addiction sets in.

It's certainly possible that much substance abuse among otherwise well adjusted teenagers is actually part of a quest to feel better. If your teenager has displayed some symptoms of depression, and then becomes secretive and rebellious, this is a red flag. You must investigate for possible substance abuse, and seek diagnosis and treatment for possible depression. It's essential to treat the depression and avoid the potential for your child to turn to dangerous and addictive substances, which then launches a pattern of deception.

Schizophrenia

Tragically, schizophrenia, a serious mental illness, tends to develop in late adolescence. We see evidence of this disease in our mental institutions and, sadly, among the chronically homeless population on our streets. The disease is characterized by distorted thought processes and losing touch with reality. Left untreated, schizophrenic individuals can't function in society, and may become anxious, paranoid, and sometimes prone to violent acting out. The onset may be linked to use of hallucinatory drugs, which is one reason that it is so critical to monitor your children and keep them away from these substances.

Obsessive-compulsive disorder (OCD)

OCD is not specifically associated with teenagers, but it can develop during adolescence (and even in young children). The easiest way to describe it is to think of people who repeat an activity again and again. Some may wash their hands over and over because they have developed a fear of germs. Or they constantly look out of the window and check the street for potential criminals—they may have become obsessed with the idea that thieves are on the loose. Some individuals with OCD may place items in their home with exactitude, such as measuring the distance between the lamp and the edge of a table, always alert for any sign that the placement has changed.

OCD is often related to other conditions, such as depression. I mention it here because it may develop in teens who use drugs and alcohol and may be self-medicating to try to relieve their symptoms of OCD or depression. Furthermore, they might start obsessing about where they'll get the substances they abuse. Again, in teens, the ongoing quest to find drugs and alcohol is by definition an exercise in deception. The anxiety and furtiveness associated with this search can transform into obsessive behavior.

I've listed these diseases, not to needlessly scare you, but rather to increase your awareness of the kinds of diseases that can make your child vulnerable to risky behaviors and, by association, deception.

Chapter 9

The Big Lies and What You Can Do about Them

Based on the research I discussed earlier in this book, we know for sure that a large number of teenagers will cheat on tests if they believe they can get away with it; if challenged, they will lie about having cheated. It all flows together: Deceptive behavior leads to lying about the deceptive behavior—and then there's the rush of getting away with it.

When you consider the kind of lies you're watching for, would cheating on tests make it on the list? It's possible that you would have missed it. Few parents imagine that cheating is so widespread. Perhaps we assume that the monitoring is tight and cheaters are generally caught, thereby deterring this particular form of deception.

What else might we miss if we're not paying attention and thinking creatively? I've listed some key areas in which deception is common and offer ways to prevent or detect it. I use the broad term "deception," because sneaking around, omitting key information, and covering one's tracks may not be outright lies, but they are strategies designed to deceive.

When you're aware of areas in which lies are likely to take place, you can plan a "counter-offensive" and have the means of detection available to you. The list below gives some examples of the areas in which it's important to monitor behavior and be skeptical. Most of all though, create clear rules and, with follow-through, reduce the occasion for lies.

Location, location, location

Left to their own devices during conversations about where they are or have been, teens would become vague or claim their supposed right to privacy. You probably remember the classic exchange that summed up the teen years:

Parent: *Where did you go?*

Teen: *Out.*

Parent: *What did you do?*

Teen: *Nothing.*

Teens will lie about their location usually in order to cover up other activities. We need only think back to our own youth to verify that. Most of us recall times that we claimed to be at a friend's house, but we were really somewhere else. Lies about location may start fairly early in childhood, especially if verification and monitoring are lacking. On the other hand, if your children enter their teen years knowing that you will keep track of their whereabouts, they'll likely understand that you will take away privileges if they are caught in lies about where they went and with whom.

When teens become old enough to drive, they will push the limits based on how much freedom they believe they have. But it isn't unusual for teenagers to take their cars to places their parents have placed off limits. Tragically, teens tend to show bad judgment about speeding, too. This is a difficult area to monitor, but not as difficult as it once was.

If you live in an area where your teenager must drive to get to school and to a job then you may be uneasy with the degree of freedom he or she has. You may trust your child, but not 100%. Technology has provided some tools to help you, including a GPS (global positioning system) you can place on your car. GPS technology can be a way to monitor your child's location and speed in the car. You can install this system on the car without your child's knowledge. I don't know that this is necessary if you monitor your child's use of the car in other ways, perhaps checking mileage and such, simply as a way to remind your teens that you are watching. (Sometimes that's all it takes to keep them honest.) Fairly new on the market are cell phones with GPS technology (location-finder phones).

You can also keep tabs on your child's location in old-fashioned ways, namely by checking up. Is there actually a party at a certain friend's home, and are the kids sure the parents will be there? Teenagers may lie about these things routinely, but they will give up if they know their parents intend to check on the circumstances surrounding this party. The same rules can apply to school events.

Curfews certainly help, and asking your teen about their evenings helps establish accountability. Your child will understand that he or she cannot slip into the house unnoticed, but must check in with you before going to his or her room. Your teen will call you nosy, but so what?

When our daughter, Marissa, went to a high school dance, we heard about pre- and post-dance parties. Our solution to making sure that the dance was the main event involved teaming up with her date's parents. They drove the teens to the dance and then came to our house to socialize with us for the evening. This way, the teens were dropped off and picked up, and both sets of parents established the time. We were able to prevent them from adding free-wheeling parties to an evening at a school dance. So enlist other parents to help you handle the location issue.

In our family, we decided against allowing sleepovers and slumber parties, and we've extended this policy into the teenage years. We reserve weekends as family time, and that's when these events generally are scheduled. As children become teens, these overnight parties can become occasions for drinking and drugs, along with sexual activity. Teens tend to lie about parents being home, so any overnight activity requires discussion with the host parents and verification of time and location.

Details are important. Learn the "who, what, when, and where" of every evening out, every school event, and all social occasions. This is part of keeping track of your teen's whereabouts.

What are the consequences? The punishment for violating your rules about location can involve location. For example, teenagers don't like being grounded, which to them is essentially "house arrest." As your teenagers get older, they will want more time on their own with friends, but if they can't be trusted to be truthful about it, then grounding them is a direct, cause and effect, punishment.

The internet
Limiting hours spent on the computer can help reduce the occasion to lie. If you're monitoring your children's homework, then you will know what needs to be done on the computer, and when it's complete, you can decide how much additional time is allowed. For example, we allow our teenager to email her friends, but we

don't allow text messaging on her phone. After our son Jack finishes his homework on the computer, he can visit one of the sites to check the sports scores he likes to follow. The history feature on web browsers allows parents to easily check on recent activity. That's how I detected a lie that Jack told about getting right down to his homework when he'd actually gone to one of these sports sites first.

The consequences of violating computer use rules: If you are concerned that your teenager is already involved in online activities you don't approve of, you can change the rules about Internet use in your household. This could involve limiting time on the computer, prohibiting chat room visits, and so on. To verify that the new rules are being followed, you can buy undetectable computer monitoring software. This program saves information on your child's computer, and you can retrieve it and find out where the child has been—a different kind of location monitoring.

Your child's safety is the key reason to set firm rules about the computer. Keeping track of the way your household computer is used can help you enforce the rules and prevent the computer from encroaching on family time. However, an equally valid reason to limit online activity is the time it consumes. Too many children (and adults) wile away hours on the computer rather than reading or spending time with family and friends.

A related issue
As I said earlier, I don't believe children of any age should have televisions in their rooms. First, this sets up occasions to lie about what they're watching. Frankly, cable premium channels aside, even the family hour TV dramas often show nearly explicit sexuality. (Daytime soap operas may be questionable as well.) While you can't protect your children from all less-than-valuable televi-

sion, you have a better chance of controlling what they watch if the television is in a common family area. I'm not suggesting that television is a bad or evil medium. In fact, for entertainment and enrichment, it has great value. Teenagers need downtime, too, so I'm not talking about forbidding all TV.

Drugs, alcohol, and sex

As you can see, I put these together because they often go together, and we could consider them "the big three." It's a rare teen who experiments with drugs and alcohol but doesn't violate the sexual standards you have set. These are areas in which you must go to every length to prevent the harmful effects of engaging in any of these things. In addition, if your children are looking for ways to drink and use drugs, they will lie. The more they use these substances, the more they will lie. Similarly, if they are moving toward sexual activity, they will try to cover it up.

Monitoring your teenagers for substance abuse will quickly bring on complaints about and accusations of nagging. Teenagers, both male and female, also consider their sexual activity their own business. That may be the case when your children go off to college or enlist in the military or find jobs after high school graduation and move away, but it is your business while they're in your home. You set the standards for your family, and I'd recommend being clear in your own mind about what they are. Parents vary in their reasons for setting sexual boundaries; some base them on moral codes, others on the dangers of contracting sexually transmitted diseases or becoming pregnant or impregnating a partner. I also recommend being clear that your expectations apply to both sexes.

In general, young people who are focused on their goals and who are planning for the future are less likely to stray into drugs and alcohol in their teenage years. (College-age teens are a different story.

Almost all older teens will drink alcohol on college campuses.) As I've said before, it's a critical part of your job as a parent to keep your high-school-age teenagers away from alcohol and drugs.

The consequences of violating your rules about the "big three"

The consequences for underage drinking or drug use can be anything from grounding to counseling, depending on many factors. If you believe your child has just begun to stray into these forbidden areas, you may nip it in the bud by removing privileges, then returning them gradually if he or she shows understanding of how serious this behavior is.

Some families institute home drug and alcohol testing. For example, breathalyzers and urine drug testing are available options. This has tended to be a controversial area, and at one time I might have believed that this testing was going too far and was a violation of privacy. Since becoming a parent, however, I have modified my stance on teenagers' rights to privacy and believe that privacy in this age group is not an automatic right. In a sense, we mature into the right to privacy, and it doesn't come automatically. It may not be fully "operative" until our children are financially independent and out on their own.

If your child has shown a pattern of alcohol and drug use, don't wait to get help, because an addiction may be developing. Seek counseling, and, most of all, don't rely on a teenager's promise not to drink or use drugs again. If an addiction has taken hold, your child will lie to keep on using. Deception and lying are part of the addict's profile.

If you discover sexual activity of which you don't approve, you may decide to cut back your child's ability to date at all or you may decide to increase the level of monitoring. This is a family issue, and you must make your beliefs clear to both your sons and daughters.

Have you determined what your dating rules entail? This is an area in which it's difficult to determine what constitutes a violation of the rules, because the range of activity is so broad.

Sexual promiscuity is another matter, and teenagers of both sexes who are involved with multiple sexual partners are at high risk for contracting sexually transmitted diseases and becoming pregnant. School performance and family life suffer, too. Without question, promiscuous teens will lie about what they're up to, and they will distance themselves from their parents. Promiscuity may indicate problems with self-esteem and possibly substance abuse. I strongly suggest you seek help to deal with this issue. Punishment alone is not going to get to the root of this problem.

Teenagers may or may not see any advantage in trying to hide information about these two areas. They tend to view these issues as situational. For example, teenagers who are responsible and goal-oriented in many areas may need to be hounded about cleaning their rooms or tending to their laundry. They may disappear into their rooms when it's time to mow the lawn or unload the dishwasher. It's difficult to get away with deception in these areas because they can easily get caught in lies when their rooms aren't cleaned or dishes are left piled up in the sink. When it comes to these issues, the worst that can happen is that parents feel like nags.

Money and chores

Families vary in their policies about money. I would reduce the occasion to lie by monitoring how children spend it. When they have part-time jobs, I believe parents are entitled to require them to put a certain percentage of the money they've earned into a college or post-graduation fund.

If you note that your teenager needs a great deal of cash, then I'd probe to find a reason why he or she needs it. Parents often say that they first realized their teenagers were using drugs when they began to make up all kinds of reasons that they needed money. I also believe that having too much disposable income promotes poor choices, which is why I believe in setting a policy about saving money earned. Families may also decide that money earned be applied to a particular expense, such as car insurance. Some families have an allowance system, some give money out on an as-needed basis. But overall, how kids spend money is your business as a parent.

Taking Action

When it comes to telling lies, your most important job is to detect deception and jump in quickly to correct the situation. Monitoring your children is harder than letting things slide, but harmony is overrated if the alternative is allowing your child to slip into bad habits.

The actions you take today have implications for the physical and emotional wellbeing of your children. Beyond that, deception has a negative impact on the atmosphere in your home, and undermines family unity and the kind of family you want to create.

Chapter 10

Preventing Lies with Family Values

I deliberately use the term "family values," even though it is usually associated with conservative politics and even some religious views. In other words, it's a buzz word that ends up igniting controversy and potentially nasty exchanges about who has better family values. However, here, I'm taking the term out of the realm of controversial politics and religion and reclaiming the term for all families.

I've used the term for a simple reason: every family is responsible for establishing its value system and passing it on to its children. For some families, religious beliefs may form the basis of their value systems, and religious worship and study are regular features of their family lives. That's a personal choice. However, I don't believe that holding any particular religious belief is necessary to live with high ethical and moral standards, and then pass these moral codes on to children.

In addition, I believe that too many parents have surrendered the primary job of teaching the values that define their families. No other institution or entity has this job. School systems, religious communities, peers, television, and popular culture are not good substitutes for parents. If you examined our society, you wouldn't know this, because of the amount of advice directed at parents about ways to manage all these outside influences. It's as if we've come to a place where we're expected to accept that these influences have real power to compete with the family. Perhaps we should be having conversations about *minimizing* the importance of the outside "noise," or at least consciously choosing what we allow in.

Currently, many parents find themselves engaged in a high-stakes quest to take back control and resist succumbing to the myriad influences on our children. I'm not sure when it happened, but parents appear to have lost a sense of their own power. We've become lax about so many things related to our children, and have allowed standards to be set by the lowest common denominator rather than elevating the principles by which we choose to live and giving them a prominent place. This shift has a direct relationship to our children's behavior and their attitudes about deception and lying.

After considerable research and study about the nature of and reasons for deception, I've concluded that the best way to avoid occasions in which lying takes place is to create a strong family unit, one in which the children learn early in life that their first allegiance is to the family. This idea of loyalty and allegiance sends the message that family time means something and loyalty goes first to the family—everything else is secondary. Friends, dating, school activities, religious groups, sports, the Internet are all of secondary importance. In the kind of value system I'm talking about, the family recognizes and reclaims its role as central and dominant in the child's life.

When my wife, Debra, and I started our family, we realized that we couldn't simply state that family is important; instead, we agreed that our value is "Family is important, and here is our family to play with." This attitude shows itself in the day-to-day atmosphere in our home and in the activities we choose. For example, rather than have our four children go their separate ways (and shuttle them around) to various activities every weekend, we spend those days together almost all the time. The whole family goes to the zoo or an amusement park or even to the store to shop as a group.

TV shows and magazines focused on parenting often cite the problem of the over-scheduled child. It's true that many parents spend hours in the car ferrying their children back and forth from soccer to play dates to swimming lessons. They spend hours on the phone arranging car pools, and then one of the parents may pick up dinner and bring it home to be consumed by the family whenever they happen to drift in. Evening hours may mean more of the same, or kids and parents may end up isolated in their private spaces. This kind of schedule works against the allegiance and commonality we've established for our family.

Several years ago, when our children were still quite young, we decided that at least during the years before high school, our first priority was to protect family time. This means that we have resisted the pressures to enroll our children in organized sports activities, which often demand rigorous after-school schedules and then consumes considerable time on the weekends as well.

We made our decision based on the belief that this kind of outside activity takes too much time away from the family. In addition, we don't want to allow coaches, park districts, or the school to take the place of our family unit. The goal of family cohesion is too important to relinquish to outside influences, even organized sports.

It seems to me that we live in the era of the "role model." We hear debates about teachers, religious leaders, coaches, sports figures, even celebrities as potential role models for our children. I hope that my children's teachers are admirable role models, for example. Teachers can inspire children and help them develop new interests and even passions about areas of knowledge that may lead to career choices. However, Debra and I do not count on them to reinforce or pass on our family values. This is true for all the adults that come in and out of our children's lives in various capacities.

I believe it's time to rethink our emphasis on and assumptions about the way we emphasize a wide range of activities that we've come to see as essential to a healthy childhood. For example, one of the rationales for enrolling young children in sports is the need for physical activity—old fashioned exercise. As a doctor, I urge parents to make sure that their children engage in more physical activity. However, how did organized sports for seven- or eight-year-olds (or even younger) become the answer? This strikes me as another example of transferring solutions to problems away from the family and into the hands of various outside experts.

Sometimes it seems that we're often presented with two choices, an either-or proposition to numerous problems. Childhood obesity is a growing problem; therefore, we can either let our kids keep watching TV and living their sedentary lifestyles or we can enroll them in organized sports. What's wrong here? What about the other choices? Could we limit TV? Could we go for family bike rides in the summer? Could we go to the community swimming pool as a family? Do we need to enroll our children in swimming classes, or can we teach them to swim? Children can play with their siblings or neighborhood children in the backyard or in nearby parks. Almost everyone will agree that when left to play in self-organized groups, or with a sibling or two, children tend to be active and creative.

Some would argue that at any age, organized activities, such as sports, teach certain important values as well as promoting fitness. While this is true to an extent, we don't need other people to teach our children manners and sportsmanship. In addition, relying on the school or park district to keep your child fit is analogous to relying on *Sesame Street* to teach your child language. It doesn't make sense.

Changing the Emphasis

In addition to keeping our children safe and healthy, our biggest job as parents involves shepherding our children through their character-development years and instilling the attitudes, values, and skills that will help guide them through life. We also must establish the priorities that will help them move forward to independence. For this reason, our family puts academics before outside activities, including TV and the Internet. It's also the reason we don't allow our 15-year-old to text message her friends (a huge time-waster), for example, or allow our children to have television sets and computers in their rooms. As I mentioned earlier, keeping TV and computers in common areas and out in the open reduces the occasion to lie.

Since we place high value on academics, we set up the household to accommodate that value. We monitor homework and check the finished product. Our children's schools don't tolerate unexplained absences, so if one of my children decided to skip school, we would always find out immediately. This eliminates another occasion in which deception occurs among some teens. A zero-tolerance policy is not uniform across the country, however, so I suggest that you find out the way your children's schools handle absences. Will you always find out if even one class is skipped? Will the school call you? Again, if academic achievement is your priority, then make sure you are aware of all the policies, and rules, and regulations in your child's school.

Just Say No—It's Just Not Enough

Drugs and alcohol and early sexual activity threaten our children's safety and welfare, and they happen to be areas in which they tend to tell lies. Here again, parents must eliminate or limit the occasions when teenagers can go astray in these areas. Without question, parents are responsible for educating their children about these dangers. However, I want my children to have a broad education about drugs, alcohol, and sex, so I approve of schools having a role. I don't believe that abstinence-only sex education is wise, but neither do I believe that it's wise to allow dating teenagers too much time alone and unsupervised.

Research shows that much of teen sexual activity occurs during the hours between the end of the school day and the dinner hour, when parents return home. Given this reality, we can conclude that teens shouldn't be unsupervised after school. Perhaps one of the parents can arrange his or her work schedule to be home at that time. Or single parents can work out a strategy to help each other out and cover those hours. In other words, if parents put a value on sexual abstinence in their teens and also are determined to keep them away from addictive substances, then send that message in the strongest possible terms.

Parents probably have many allies among other parents, who also value family time and want to discourage a variety of potentially dangerous activities. Unfortunately, too many parents fail to tap this great resource—each other. I suggest reaching out to other parents and forming the kind of partnership that promotes wholesome activities and safety. Find out what rules the parents of your teenager's friends set in their households, and make sure they're compatible with your rules. Let these other adults know what you expect from your children.

Just as privacy for teenagers is an illusion these days, so is the concept of freedom without follow-up and verification, which is why you need rules and the means to enforce them. Rather than turning over your power as a parent to outside influences, such as the school, a religious institution, or friends, enlist their help—turn them into allies to reinforce the values you're trying to instill.

Family as the New Religion

At one time, communities shared values common to their shared religion. However, over time, the role of religion has receded, and we live in communities that accommodate a variety of religious and secular customs and values. We've run into problems because, rather than the family stepping in to replace religion or augment its role, we've allowed myriad outside influences to take over, and no one is in the driver's seat setting the course. This is why so many parents, teachers, coaches, clergy, physicians, psychologists, and others feel that we've lost control of our children. After years of rising rates of addiction and teen pregnancy, high and unimproved dropout rates in high schools, crime rates that fluctuate very little, and rocketing divorce rates, I believe that parents are in the process of reversing the tide.

Today, parents realize that the family's moral teaching is more significant in a child's life than a religion's moral teaching and offers greater power to override the noise of unwholesome popular culture. While being active in a church, temple, or mosque may have value, it should become part of the fabric of the family's life, rather than superseding the family's moral code.

I wrote this book in part from a desire to add my voice to help families find solutions in this confusing and transitional era. I want to reinforce the guideline that parents must establish the moral code in their family and help their children internalize it. The more cohesive the family unit is, the more likely it is that the children will adopt the family mores, and the more honest the children will be. In the end, your family's moral code is the greatest gift you can give to your child.

References

Hirsch, A. R. 2003. Physical and verbal signs of lying. *Directions in Psychiatry* 23: 15–19.

Hirsch, A. R., and C. J. Wolf. 1999. A case example utilizing practical methods for detecting mendacity. *Program and Abstracts on New Research, American Psychiatric Association* (May): 208.

Hirsch, A. R., and C. J. Wolf. 2001. Practical methods for detection of mendacity: A case study. *The Journal of the American Academy of Psychiatry and the Law* 29(4): 438–44.

Hirsch, A. R., and J. J. Gruss. 1998. How successful are malingerers? Dissimulating olfactory dysfunction. *Journal of Neurological and Orthopaedic Medicine and Surgery* 18: 154–60.